Tai Chai!

Lessons for success in MLM

BOOK 1

From beginner to first basic level of success

Eddy Chai

ISBN 0-9549566-0-5
Cover design by Denise Clark
Copyright © 2003 by Eddy Chai
Published by No Limits Publications
Tel: +44 (0)1600 740146, email: john@qlsgroup.com

Chinese version published in Taiwan by China Times Group
Business Culture & Publishing Co. Ltd
Tel: (02) 2338-0861, email: jangcilu@mail.chinatimes.com.tw

Eddy's email address eddy@eddychai.com
Eddy's website address www.eddychai.com

Dedication

I would like to take a moment to thank all the countless outstanding individuals who have influenced my career: from the motivational speakers, whose work and wisdom I have enjoyed courtesy of their tapes, books and seminars; through to my many friends, who have told me so many wonderful stories over the years, which I now plan to share with you in my books. A very special thanks to Rex Maughan – if greatness stems from vision, application, focus, effort, commitment and a desire to make a contribution, then this man has these qualities, in quantities above any person I have ever met. I am forever grateful for the opportunity he gave me to study the operations of how a MLM company should be run. I have been his student and he has balanced my education.

I also have to thank John Curtis and my son for their input in writing this book, because without their input, you would be reading English which I sometimes do not even understand. I am Chinese, born in Malaysia, educated in English but when I talk about an English education, it was one learnt on the island of Borneo, the land of headhunters and where my teachers had themselves only finished High School.

– Eddy Chai

Editor's Preface

Just over a decade ago, something remarkable happened at a point in my life where I had been in Network Marketing for 3 years, with the 12 years before that in Direct Sales. I honestly thought that I'd already seen and met the best that the industry had to offer, but attending an Eddie Chai training changed my views in a heartbeat. It was apparent that he was someone enjoying huge success in Network Marketing but more importantly, one who really knew how it all worked, with total and unshakeable belief, and who was freely prepared to share with others, all that he knew and believed in.

Since that time, our paths have crossed a number of times each year and with it a growing friendship but I doubt that he is aware of just how big an influence he has been in the development of my own multi-million turnover business.

One of my main objectives in editing this book has been for meaning and clarity to take precedence over exactitudes of grammar – after all, this book is intended as a 'how to' for networkers and would-be networkers. I extend heartfelt thanks to my friend and colleague Robert Symes, for his input of technical know-how and patience in helping get this book into printable format but I alone take responsibility for any errors in grammar, punctuation or lack of meaning.

Eddy Chai - the greatest Network Marketer in the world? Arguable perhaps, except to the members of his network organization and those who have experienced his remarkable training, system and techniques. Many readers of this book may never experience his talents first hand, but within these pages everyone can now have in their possession his collected knowledge and wisdom. Read on and enjoy the fruits of success which will surely flow from diligent application.

John Curtis

Table of Contents

Introduction

For many years I had always been very unenthusiastically biased against Multi-Level-Marketing (MLM). You see, I had the misconception that it was a door-to-door business, where people had to go around knocking on doors, selling detergents and cosmetics. At the age of 25, after leaving the Malaysian Police Force as an Inspector, I became an entrepreneur. I was relatively successful and by the age of 30 made money on 4 restaurants, 2 grocery stores, 6 homes and was worth about a quarter-of-a-million dollars. Now there can be a big difference between being worth a quarter-of-a-million on paper, and having a quarter-of-a-million in the bank. I was fortunate to belong to the latter when I got involved in this amazing industry called Multi-Level-Marketing, or Network Marketing.

...I had the misconception that MLM was a door to door business...

Sometime in the summer of 1980, a nice looking gentleman was paying his bill, when he asked me if I liked making money. I did not know Calvin Carr well but his parents were regular customers of mine, and I replied that, as a businessman, of course I would be interested in making money. He then told me that he would like to discuss a business opportunity with me. Now, this man was always well dressed and I had originally assumed that he was involved in real estate. Back then, I owned six properties in a very exclusive area in the Lower Mainland of British Columbia, Canada. In fact, I was the largest property owner in that beach peninsula. Many years ago, that area was only accessible to Caucasians, and a Chinese person like me could not even have entered the gates of Crescent Beach.

I also owned the only café restaurant at the Ocean Park Mall, a place where even if you did not know anything about the restaurant business, you could still make money, as there was no competition. I worked six days a week, from 6.30 in the morning to 9.30 at night and as a result, I was able to save 60% to 70% of what I made every month. What could a person do after 9.30 pm in a retirement area with only about 20,000 people? Looking into real estate deals became a hobby and so when my upline-to-be, Calvin, approached me, I thought he was going to talk to me about real estate. Little did I know he was going to talk to me about Amway. We made an appointment to talk after I closed shop that evening.

When he came back and I saw him parking his car, I waited for him at the door. He alighted and picked up a big briefcase from the trunk of his car. When I saw that case, I thought to myself, "My, that is a lot of real estate." I was excited. After all, how was I supposed to know there was soap inside? I made coffee and sat down, smiling, ready for the great real estate deals he was going to offer. He

I lost my smile and nearly took back the coffee!

began and told me he was going to tell me about the greatest opportunity in the world, the world of Amway. I lost my smile and nearly took back the coffee!

I must really thank my then future upline for the curiosity approach he used, because if he had told me upfront that it was Amway, I would never have given him a chance. At that time, I thought I knew all about MLM, as my neighbor and several of my customers were involved in the industry, and one of my sisters and her husband were with another company, Shaklee. I had even refused to listen to a presentation from them, when they wanted to show me the business at my home.

When I heard it was Amway, I told Cal, "I'm not interested and besides, I have no time." It's funny how many prospects immediately become 'not interested in making money' and 'have no time,' when they learn that it is MLM, or think that they know all about MLM, just because their neighbor or relative is involved in the industry. Calvin replied, "Eddy, I'm already here, so will you give me one hour of your time?" Now as a Chinese, culturally I really couldn't say "no" to his request, since it was ME who had invited Cal to come and tell me about this money making opportunity that was going to make me rich. So I told him, "OK but hurry up about it." I was doing pretty well for myself at the time and thought the very idea of 'selling soap door-to-door' was beneath me.

That one hour turned into four and when I got home that night, I could not sleep. I had the habit of throwing the name cards of customers into the drawer underneath my restaurant cash register, and using rubber bands to tie them up into bundles when there were too many. At around 4.30am that Sunday morning, I drove back to my restaurant to get those name cards and started my prospect list.

On the following Monday, I jokingly told my customers that I was going to sell my restaurant and go into another business. A real estate agent by the name of Scotty was in the restaurant at the time and asked if I would let him sell the place for me. Ever since I had started my real estate hobby, all my properties were handled by Ted Crosby, a friend of mine. I told Scotty this and he replied that he understood, but promised he could sell the place in a week, and that if he couldn't, I should go ahead and place the sale with Ted. That sounded like a very fair offer, so I signed the agreement with him, but I did not believe he could do it in that time-frame. Two hours later, he 'phoned me back and told me to wait for him in the restaurant, as he'd already sold the place. Only two hours! When he came back, I was excited and amazed and asked him who had bought the place. Scotty replied, "I did." I guess when you have the only restaurant in Ocean Park, it can be sold quite easily but selling it to the real estate agent who handles the deal, is quite another thing.

Two hours later...he'd already sold the place

I met up with Cal again on Tuesday, as I wanted to commit full-time in the business. When he learnt that I'd sold my restaurant and was going full-time, Cal explained that Amway was opening in Taiwan that November, and asked if I would like to go there to do the business. I was born in Malaysia, not Taiwan, had never been to Taiwan and did not know anyone there. On top of that, I had been educated in English and did not speak or understand Mandarin. Now when I talk of an English education, it is one learnt on the island of Borneo, the land of headhunters and where my teachers had themselves only finished High School. Cal told me, "Don't worry, you are Chinese like the Taiwanese and everyone in Taiwan speaks English."

I was in for a surprise! It's true, when I arrived, yes, everyone did speak English. Three words, "No speak English."

...everyone did speak English. Three words, "No speak English."

In the September I arrived in Taiwan with my family, my upline Cal, his wife and their daughter, and we set up a center. Amway opened as planned on November 6th 1980 and we got down to work. In spite of the language difficulties, I went on to become one of Amway's biggest distributors and when I left after 6 years, my organization accounted for one third of the business in Taiwan, with over one hundred thousand distributors.

During my time with Amway, I also made an investment that didn't turn out so well, when I built the White Rock Public Market. I lost it all, and more! In the light of this experience, today I am very proud of my success and accomplishments, because every possession I now have is the fruit of my work in MLM. So when I tell you that this industry can be a vehicle to your dreams, I mean it with every fiber in my body. I am not a theory guy. I teach what I have

...every possession I now have is the fruit of my work in MLM

done and more importantly, what I am still doing. I want to be the best I can be in this business, and plan to spend the rest of my life working to discover all of its secrets, and I know I can do it.

So to those of you facing challenges in your business, I would urge you to keep focus. You may never have to face the obstacles I faced in this business; illiterate in Chinese, friendless, and broke. I have been there, seen just about everything, but nonetheless kept my focus and built one of the biggest organizations on this planet. At the end of 2002, my group organization amounted is over 1,088,249 distributorships, and that is just for Taiwan!

The main reason I am one of the best in this business, is because I decided to be a very good student. I invest a lot of time: listening to tapes; attending meetings, rallies, training courses; and reading books. I also set very high standards for myself as a speaker and trainer, but more importantly, as a responsible upline to my growing organization. Almost before I knew it, I began to create a name for myself in the industry. Today my entire organization has over 2 million distributors and has expanded to over 25 countries, including Taiwan, USA, Canada, UK, Malaysia, Philippines, Singapore, France, New Zealand, Spain, South Africa, India, China, Indonesia, Australia and Hong Kong. In 1998, I was recognized as one of the outstanding businessmen of the year in Taiwan. I quickly acquired a few pleasant nick names, like 'The MLM Guru', 'The Taiwan Legend', 'The Teacher' and even a rather outrageous one, 'The God of MLM'. I thank all of you for your respect and all these kind compliments, but what I really like to be called is, "Eddy Chai, a good student."

Over the years, I was approached by two authors who wanted to help me write my autobiography, but I turned them down, because there are many people whose lives are much more colorful than mine. **More importantly, I already had another plan.** After joining MLM in 1980, I was introduced to a book called 'Think and Grow Rich' by Napoleon Hill. It took the author 25 years to write a perfect book. I have set my goal that I too will one day write an MLM book, and like Napoleon Hill, will do it only after studying the business for over 20 years. I want it to be a perfect MLM book.

Today, May 8th 2003, is the birthday of my youngest son Isaac and I have chosen this day, to start to put my final work together. A couple of years shy of Napoleon Hill's time frame so that if it is not perfect, I have an excuse. However, I want all of you to know that this book was started way back in 1980, and my goal is to give you a perfect MLM book. I want to give you a business system and when I am finished, you will not be left wondering what that system is. The pages I will share with you have been my manual, guiding me over the years. These books will teach you, "What to do" as well as, "How to do it."

I want my books to be able to help leaders learn to be great network marketers and speakers; where any leader can take any topic, master it and be a great speaker on that topic; where even from my first volume, Book 1, any new leader, after mastering all fourteen training notes, will be a leader as good as one in the business for over 10 years; where any leader who can master even half of all the training notes I put together in all three books, should become one of their country's most outstanding MLM leaders. Many people make MLM a profession, yet how many leaders do you know, who can give training lessons on fourteen different topics? It is a fact that Multi Level Marketers

> *It is a fact that Multi Level Marketers are some of the most unprofessional people in the world*

are some of the most unprofessional people in the world. If doctors were as unprofessional as we are, I wonder how many sick people could ever hope to leave hospital alive. All too often, we behave like sailors who do not know how to swim.

Purpose

One day, one of the strongest leaders in my organization told me that one of her downlines had given a great training. When asked how she knew it was great, she responded that her downline had spoken very well and got all her facts right. I told her that any

...any training is only great, if it is suitable for the audience

training is only great, if it is suitable for the audience. A great presentation given on an advanced topic to a group of beginners, or an elementary topic to a group of experienced leaders, is a bad training, no matter how well it is presented.

Over the years, I observed a few facts:

1. All very big and strong organizations are so, because the top leaders are very strong speakers and motivators. In the MLM industry, we are paid to be communicators, but you cannot be a great communicator if you do not know what, or how, to communicate.

2. There are many topics that need to be taught to an organization.

3. There are no training manuals to cover most of these topics.

4. No writer has divided these topics, so that that they are suitable for their appropriate distributor level. No one book has been scripted to help leaders and trainers, so that they do not give the wrong training to the different groups in their organization.

From these observations, I set out to put together, 'Tai Chai – Lessons for Success in MLM.' This is an accumulation of over 20 years worth of the same training material I give to my organization. It consists of three books:

Book 1 - suitable for beginners to the first basic level of success.

Book 2 - suitable for leaders who have developed one to three separate 'legs' (lines where groups of distributors are growing).

Book 3 - suitable for the higher 'pin' positions on company Marketing or Compensation Plans; group leaders and very high pins.

Read all these books diligently and learn how to do MLM properly, but more importantly, become a great trainer, giving the right training to your organization and carrying on my work and contribution to this industry. To be a great trainer, you must have facts, teach skills and sell ideas. I will also try and give you lots of great stories I have learnt over the years, so

> *To be a great trainer, you must have facts, teach skills and sell ideas*

that you can make your training fun and interesting. In doing so, do not forget that we do not tell stories just for fun. Observe their purpose and why they are told.

I would like to take the opportunity at this time, to address a few words to owners of MLM companies and their management. Please do step back once in a while, to check on yourself and the knowledge you possess. Is it up to standard? Over the years, as both a multi level marketer and consultant, I have met quite a number of you, or distributors from your companies, and listened to horror stories. Sometimes, I only need to read a company policy manual or to study its marketing plan, to see the knowledge you possess. I am sorry to tell you that on a scale of 1 to 10, the majority will be lucky to be rated a 5. Of course, I doubt you believe my assessment of you, as you own the company and may have made a lot of money from it, resulting in your thinking that you are an amazing genius. Trust me, most of you will not make a 5 and even the better ones, would be lucky to get a 7. If I gave you a proficiency test, by asking you 10 advanced questions about MLM, I doubt most of you could even give a decent answer to half of them. Most of you probably do not even know how to give a proficient presentation of your company's marketing plan in front of a big audience. Please, I expect you to be an 8 or 9 and if it sounds as though I am coming down hard on you, it is only because I want you to accept responsibility in handling the livelihood of distributors who believe in you. Please do not lie to yourself that you are genius, while knowing at the back of your mind that it is not true.

Another observation is that most leaders and organizations do not have a system of training, and as a result, their growth is stunted. Often their system runs along the lines of, "Keep it simple", "Work hard" and "Stay excited". Slogans and attitudes like these are essential in helping people succeed in Network Marketing, but they are not the actual working methodologies, activities or ways of working and in common with their organizations, I am often left wondering what their system actually is.

It is very important that all group leaders introduce a business building system to their downlines, so as to ensure smooth, fast and permanent growth. As a group, leaders in Los Angeles must teach the same things as leaders in Chicago. You must have a system, and at the same time, a good group leader must lead distributors away from doing the business by trial and error. A good leader must never teach what they **THINK** is the right answer for a situation but rather, what **IS** the right answer. If you do not yet have a system, or you are the owner of a new company, please feel free to use my system. I would like to especially encourage owners of new companies to do so, as you are playing with the livelihood of distributors who believe in you. A Network Marketing business should be much like all the international franchise corporations, operating exactly the same way in every area, region or country, according to standardized procedures and training. Any distributor visiting a new area, region or country, will thus feel completely at home, because everything is run exactly the same. You need not tell your people it is Eddy Chai's system, because this is not my system, but rather the MLM system I have learnt over the last 20 years, as to how MLM should be done.

> *...a good group leader must lead distributors away from doing the business by trial and error*

And now I need your help. I told you before that my purpose is to write a perfect MLM book, so as you read and use what I have written, I would like your input. If you find a mistake, disagree, find certain things that you think are wrong, or have a new idea or an improvement that can be made on a topic, please write to me, and together we will perfect this work, leaving a legacy for distributors who come after us. Here are my email and website addresses. eddy@eddychai.com, www.eddychai.com

I have often heard people say that there is no true right answer for certain challenges in our business. I disagree. I believe those who say things like this either do not know the answers, or have not yet learnt enough. We are in this business together, and must all do our part and the right thing, giving our individual input for the betterment of an industry that many of us are committed to, forever. Please help me, so that by the year 2010, my thirtieth year in MLM, we will have a perfect book that we wrote together.

How to use this book if you are a trainer

KISS = Keep It Simple Special

a) Bear in mind that the people you are training are beginners.

b) Refrain from going into difficult advanced information, as this is only Book 1.

c) Do not be too hard or demanding on your audience, but be firm and give instructions as to what you want to get done.

d) Make it fun. Be funny. Tell Stories.

I have done a summary at the end of every lesson, and I advise every trainer not to do any training without one. If you use a computer in your presentation, I have also done a Power Point summary that you can download for free from my website. You can add your own stories and other extra information that you may wish to use, or remove some of my points that you may not want to talk about during your training.

LEADER'S INCANTATION

I AM A LEADER

I WILL BELIEVE, NOT DOUBT

I WILL BUILD AND CREATE

I WILL LEARN AND TEACH

I WILL LEAD BY EXAMPLE

I WILL KEEP MY FOCUS

I WILL AIM HIGHER

I AM A FORCE FOR GOOD

I AM THE MASTER OF MY EMOTIONS

SEE YOU AT THE TOP

From beginner to first basic level of success

"Far better it is to dare mighty things, to win glorious triumphs even though checkered by failure, than to rank with those poor spirits who neither enjoy nor suffer much because they live in the gray twilight that knows neither victory nor defeat."

Theodore Roosevelt

Lesson 1
Why you cannot fail in MLM

1. Introduction

Facts about financial freedom

It is a fact that if you want to attain financial freedom, you must be involved in an occupation that is going to allow you to do so. I have got nothing against working for a living, but you must understand that a job (**J**ust **O**ver **B**roke) is just for surviving, and not for the creation of wealth. If you want to be wealthy, you must never make working for others a life-long endeavor. To dream that you will one day become wealthy, when you are an employee in a bank, is most likely just a dream. Instead, you might want to consider robbing the bank! At least there is then the possibility that you may be wealthy! If you are not in one already, you need to be in a business of your own, and MLM is definitely the most accessible route, and for many, their only choice.

MLM may be the only vehicle to your dreams

However, many people still do not realize that this is the new millennium and that many drastic changes have taken place in the business world over the past few decades. These changes are affecting the lives and options of everyone within the entire economic structure. In his book, 'Only the Paranoid Survive', Andy Grove, former CEO of Intel, calls these events 'Strategic Inflection Points'; seismic shifts in the rules of the game or sometimes, the rule book being completely re-written. As a result, increasing numbers of small and medium businesses are facing challenges that are threatening their survival, because the rules have changed. It is time for people to 'wake up and smell the coffee' and to realize that MLM may be the only vehicle to their dreams. It is time for them to take MLM seriously and put forward their best efforts, instead of giving up when they face obstacles or discouragement.

I cannot therefore think of a better lesson to start my training of over 40 lessons, than with this very first lesson, 'Why you cannot fail in MLM.'

2. People we meet in MLM

In the course of your business, I am sure you come across the following kinds of people:

      a) People who would not even come to a meeting.
      b) People who come but have no interest.
      c) People who join but never do anything.
      d) People who show initial interest but give up easily.

Yet many of them are looking for opportunity and are in need of a break in life. I hope that you write down what is below for these people, and then ask them what they see:

OPPORTUNITYISNOWHERE

OPPORTUNITY IS **NOWHERE**

OR

OPPORTUNITY IS **NOW HERE**

3. Two challenges faced by Multi-Level marketers

The 80% - 20% Rule

Firstly, understand that very often it is the people who need money the most, who do not know how to make money. When it comes to wealth creation, they simply do not know where to begin. It has been their habit to spend money but not to know how to make it, so even when they are presented with an opportunity, they cannot see it, nor do they know how to

4

take advantage of it.

Find a deserted island; put 100 people above the age of 25 there and then give each one $100,000. Go back to the island 5 years later, and I can guarantee, 80% of all the wealth will be in the hands of 20% of the people. It will be a good idea for you, as you read this book, to now make a decision as to which group you wish to belong!

We only have ourselves to blame

Secondly, we cannot blame some prospects for not wanting anything to do with MLM, after all the horror stories they may have heard from former distributors, or perhaps things they read from newspapers, magazines or the internet. Many times, we can only blame ourselves, as I am sure you will recognize the following:

a) Some companies are not true MLM companies but are in fact pyramid schemes, set up by unscrupulous people whose only goal is to cheat as many other people as possible. These organizations attract those foolish enough to believe that MLM is where you play the money game, not where you distribute products and services.

b) 90% of all new MLM companies will not reach their fifth birthday, all-too-often aided by dim-witted owners knowing very little about MLM, who have set up their company, doomed to failure right from the start.

c) Many leaders exaggerate their products, marketing plan and their incomes.

d) The amounts of time we spend criticizing each other, instead of respecting each other, and still we wonder, why so many people have a bad impression of our industry? We, the people inside, are telling the people outside, how rotten we are. Find a leader from a company and tell him or her about Amway, or tell a leader from Amway about another company, then sit back and observe what I mean. You are going to get an earful of negatives.

e) Please understand that MLM companies do not normally spend a lot of money on advertising. Reporters do not therefore have to worry about losing advertising revenue for their newspaper, if they write bad things about us. Let me show you an article that appeared a few years ago, in the biggest English newspaper in Taiwan, when McDonalds got into some trouble in India over their French fries. The article appeared in a small corner and only measured 5cm x 7cm, even though it concerned a serious issue, since giving a Hindu beef fat is a terrible taboo. I guarantee that if the same thing had happened to an MLM company, reporters would have written up big articles for their papers. Here is the report:

McDonald's discreetly apologizes over beef fat

NEW YORK, AFP

Fast-food leviathan McDonald's on Thursday offered a discreet excuse on its U.S. Internet Web site for failing to inform customers that it seasoned its french fries with beef fat.

The statement follows a lawsuit filed in early May in Seattle, in the northwestern state of Washington, on behalf of two Hindus and a non-Hindu vegetarian claiming the restaurant chain had lied to customers for more than a decade by using beef fat in its french fries.

However, I still want to advise all distributors and owners of MLM companies to act responsibly, and not to do things to create problems for the industry, leaving us open to attack, instead of us blaming the media.

4. The three development stages of a country

This is perhaps the most important reason why many of us have to face the fact that, 'You cannot fail in MLM.' Every country goes through three stages of development, from being under-developed to developed. What are the changes that will take place, which will affect our lives and the business world? Let us study each stage.

Under-developed country

At this stage, the country is poor and poverty prevails. There are very few white-collar jobs and business is mostly conducted by small vendors. I like to compare this stage to a tank filled with small fishes. These small fishes will compete against one another, just like small vendors compete against one another in the market place. Small capital investment is required.

Developing country

As the country progresses, huge amounts of capital are needed to build infrastructure. At the same time the government has to encourage the construction of big factories, to produce goods for export in order to earn foreign exchange. These require huge amounts of capital, something small vendors do not have. The government therefore has to encourage the establishment of big corporations, allowing selected businessmen to have their companies go public and be listed on the stock market. These corporations normally become very big and wealthy, as they can do things, get deals and have protection under the sponsorship of the government.

Developed country

After many years of progress, the nation becomes a developed country. With infrastructure done, the factories built and the people having a higher standard of living, the big conglomerates, now flush with money, will begin to go into the business sector that used to be the territory of the small vendors. The difference is that they will go into this sector in a big way, usually in partnership with established and experienced companies from other developed countries.

When you have a tank of small fish, they all survive well together, even though the slightly bigger or stronger ones may bully the weaker or smaller fish. But what happens, when you put a really big fish into the same tank? Welcome to the business world, where the big fish will eat the small fish.

5. The result in the market place

These big corporations will destroy many small and medium businesses, and even those who made money during the developing stages, may lose everything they have, because they are unable to adjust to the changing market. Some small vendors may do well, but only because they are long established and debt free; their shops are in prime areas; or they are involved in businesses that the big companies do not want.

The trend then becomes that instead of going into business for oneself, it appears more sensible just to buy shares in the listed companies or to work for them, on the principle that, "If you can't beat them, join them."

It is also arguable that MLM success, in some degree, will be bolstered by big business. How? Consider, that any big consumer business is almost always listed on a stock exchange and that as a publicly listed company, it has a goal is to increase shareholder value. To do this, the company is always under pressure to do one of two things; to cut costs and/or increase sales, with one of the ways to increase sales being to expand market share and/or enter new markets. What is going to happen to a small/medium business owner, when a Wal-Mart, Home Depot, Carrefour, B&Q or Starbucks, decides to muscle in on his/her turf? It will be like a champion lightweight, stepping into the ring to fight a champion super heavyweight. The lightweight may have the heart of a lion, but slaughter is inevitable. The same happens in business, where the small/medium business owner may have the entrepreneurial spirit, but to go toe-to-toe against a Wal-Mart will be a slaughter. But these entrepreneurs will not disappear; they still need something to fulfill their entrepreneurial spirit and they will gravitate towards MLM.

6. On the political front and taxes

Other interesting changes also happen on the political front and to the taxes people have to pay. The rise in education levels and the growth of a larger middle class in a developed country, also leads to more political action groups. Unlike 'the good old days,' politicians now face fierce competition to be elected. Because of this pressure, they cave in to the demands of the people for more welfare services and benefits, making promises in these areas, which in turn lead to corresponding higher taxes.

Well, guess who pays the most taxes? The people who work for someone else, or the big corporations with cozy political ties?

7. Facts distributors need to face

There is now little opportunity for you to be a traditional businessperson, as even established small companies face difficulties in surviving.

How can you compete...
  a) with listed companies, when they use the money they raise from the stock market to compete with you?
  b) when they buy in such large volume from the suppliers, that their selling price may be lower than your purchase price? When I had my grocery store in Canada, I would buy chicken at wholesale for $1.29 a pound and sell it for $1.89 a pound. When the big stores put chicken on special, they sold it at 99 cents a pound. I could not even get this price at wholesale.
  c) when they can give out special deals or loss leaders every week, selling at their wholesale price to attract customers to their doorstep?
  d) when they have the money to employ specialists and professional help?
  e) when they have the money to set up their stores in the best-selected locations?
  f) when they can build a 'one-stop' shopping Mall?

Most people who run small and medium-class businesses, are not afraid of hard work...they are only troubled by the fact that the rules have changed.

It will be difficult to keep up with taxes and inflation, working for other people.

Working for a wage or salary will never give financial freedom, and working for other people is like sowing seeds in other people's gardens.

The report 'Expenditures on children by families' states that for a Y2K child, factoring in for inflation, food, shelter and other necessities, it will cost a middle-income family about US$165,630 to $233,530 over the next 17 years. There were a record number of bankrupt filings in 2003; 1.5 million in the U.S. and nearly one third of those filing for bankruptcy owed an entire year's worth of their salary on their credit cards. In fact, more children endured their parents' bankruptcy in that year, than in their parents' divorce.

Globalization, the tip of the iceberg

An increasingly common household word and in the years to come, some of you will experience the meaning of this first hand.

The 3rd February, 2003 edition of Businessweek, contained an excellent article about this phenomenon. Developed countries are now experiencing the same job shift overseas for white-collar jobs, as has already happened to blue-collar manufacturing jobs. Often times, these white-collar jobs can be done overseas, 60%-70% cheaper. Back office banking, auditing, financial analysis, semiconductor chip design, aeronautical design, architecture, and call centers, are all moving overseas.

Bank of America is shifting 4,700 credit card processing and back office jobs to India. An architect charges US$18 an hour in Hungary, versus $65 in the U.S. Microsoft pledged to invest $450 million in India and $750 million in China over the three years starting in 2003. Why? Because India and China each produce more engineers than America, and Microsoft wants to tap into the country's intellectual capital. Call centers for Intel, Chevron, IBM, and American Express are moving to the Philippines, in addition to auditing and financial analysis jobs offered by the big audit firms. Boeing outsources aeronautical design to engineers in Moscow. Texas Instruments and Intel do likewise for semiconductor chip design in India, and this is just a brief summary. Do not be surprised, if Cadillacs are made in China at some future time. What is making this all possible? Digitization, the Internet, and high speed data networking. The world has suddenly become very, very small.

Globalization is lowering the income bar of developed countries, to that of the rest of the still-developing world. It's obvious who will be the winners in this exercise. Big corporations in developed countries will be able to cut costs, increase profit margins and make their shareholders happy. Countries like India, China, the Philippines and Eastern Europe will greatly benefit. So who loses out? Some might say this is not a zero sum equation and that everybody wins. Theoretically, this structural unemployment, where the Gross Domestic Product output of a country remains the same, but with less people needed, will free those now unemployed to develop and grow into new industries. Try telling that to someone, or a friend, who got axed at Bank of America.

This trend is not confined to just the United States. When Britain's empire builders so vigorously exported the English language and culture to India, it is unlikely they ever guessed that many decades later, Indian workers would use these same tools to take British jobs. The UK's Communication Workers Union has reported that up to 200,000 jobs are threatened. Tesco, Britain's leading super-market chain, plans to move 1,000 call center jobs to Bangalore. British Telecom, which pays British call center staff from £5.80 Sterling an hour, found it could provide the same customer service in India for 80% cheaper, resulting in a planned relocation of 2,200 jobs. Prudential reports that it will save US$25 million a year, by moving some of their operations to Bombay.

If you are living in a developed country, it is time to 'wake up and smell the coffee.' You should say a small prayer and thank God that there is a business called MLM. The writing is on the wall.

On the bright side?

Several big corporations use MLM as a way of marketing their products or services, and we are talking about big companies, like Colgate Palmolive, Gillette, and MCI WorldCom, etc. However, I feel it is wiser for manufacturers to market their products through a proven MLM company, as we also need to ask ourselves how well the above companies have done in their MLM endeavors? Not very well, is the answer.

The growth in MLM

Statistics given by the Direct Selling Association for their members sales worldwide, indicate that MLM grew from $10 billion in 1980 to $ 40 billion for 1992 and then to $ 70 billion by 1996.

China Post, Monday, 24th May, 1993
Direct Sales Report
'There are currently more than 30 countries that are members of the World Direct Sales Alliance, which posts annual sales revenue of around US$45 billion. Japan is the largest member of the alliance, with yearly direct sales revenue of around US$20 billion, involving 1.7 million people. The United States ranks second with an annual revenue of some US$10 billion, involving four million people.'

These are the total worldwide sales of most major MLM companies in the world, and if we just look at the United States of America for the year 2000, the combined sales of all MLM companies accounted for only US$26 billion, as against US$3 trillion from traditional businesses. This is hardly 1% of all the business done and when even compared to just Wal-Mart, it is apparent that MLM has hardly begun. Wal-Mart's sales for 2002 were US $246.4 billion; MLM's total annual sales were hardly one-month's sales for Wal-Mart! I am one of many who believe that a fair achievable goal is 3% (or about US$100 billion), just for the USA alone. As a distributor, I am happy that the industry is not yet doing as well and I hope to play a very important role to helping it achieve the potential. I challenge you to do the same, and let's all work together to make this happen, as I know this industry will also look after you. Do not make the mistake of perhaps one day regretting that you did make a decision to do this business seriously, only to see others who join later than you becoming successful.

Costs of distribution

Another plus that makes MLM increasingly viable, is the high cost of traditional distribution, with its associated high salary and rental overheads. When I had my first grocery store, 30 years ago in a poor town in East Malaysia, it was very common for me to sell things with only a 15% to 20% retail mark up. At that time, distribution cost was probably 30%, as against 70% for manufacturing. I later migrated to Vancouver, Canada, a developed country and where salary and rental levels are high and the cost of distribution exceeds that of manufacturing. Today it stands at 30% for manufacturing and 70% for distribution. As a result, it is now possible to sell many things through MLM, that we were not able to sell before. Good business sense dictates that MLM is a business model that you cannot afford to ignore.

MLM is not really opened yet in the two biggest markets

China and India account for 35% of the world's population. How well will MLM do when these two markets are opened?

Story: Many moons

An Indian brave took for himself a beautiful wife but had to leave for battle on the wedding night. Telling the wife to wait for him, before leaving for battle, he said, "Wait, me come. Must"

A year later, he came back from battle and found his beautiful wife pregnant. So he asked the wife," Many moons me no come, how come baby come?"

The wife replied, "Many moons you no come, but so many men come. How come baby no come?"

Over the years, I have seen many prospects and distributors join my organization but who after registering, were not active or left when they faced challenges. Years later, several have visited again and are always amazed at the growth in my business and how well I have done.

Some ask," Many moons me no come. You, how come money come?

I reply, "Many moons you no come, but many man come. Alex come, Mary come, John come, Thomas come. How come money no come?"

We laugh and enjoy the story but let me warn all distributors who are in the business today, not to make the same mistake. I hope I will never see the day when I meet you and you ask me, "Many moons..."

The progress made in technology

The way in which technology has progressed over the last 20 years has been phenomenal and it will also change the way we market many products in the future. The buying and selling of a whole range of products can be done now through the Internet but the question we have to ask ourselves is, what it will do to our lives in the next 20 years? Some experts are predicting that departmental stores may become future dinosaurs. While it is true that the dot-com bubble has burst and many companies went out of business, do not count them out yet. Many big departmental stores also closed, or at best have 'one foot in the grave' over this last decade. Big departmental stores like Sogo, Seibu, Woodwards, Kmart, Eatons, and the list goes on. I believe the same will happen in the Internet space. Companies like Yahoo!, Ebay, and Amazon have survived the bubble and eventually may thrive. At this time of writing, the world is being hit by a dangerous virus called SARS or Severe Acute Respiratory Syndrome. In Taipei, Taiwan, a staff member at Sogo department store was affected and as a result, the store had to be closed for 3 days in order to clean up, causing losses running into millions of dollars. Most department stores in Hong Kong and Singapore saw a crash of 50% in sales. How many businesses, I wonder, can survive a 50 % drop in business? I am more concerned, however, as to how all these changes will affect the traditional business and the small and medium business person. Will this have a domino effect on all other things? I give thanks for having an MLM business where I do not have the risks faced by traditional businesses, not least because I do not need to set up a shop.

Over the years, I have observed nearly all MLM companies setting up their own web sites, and how these sites are helping distributors in their business. Companies frequently provide a web site service to their distributors, whereby they can check their organization, order products, check sales, service customers and distributors, and even attach their own web site to the main one.

Many businesses and jobs will be phased out because of technology but it looks as though this great advancement will be a plus for those of us in MLM. I wonder at the possible future tools that technology may bring to help us in the years to come. Think for a moment about how many inventions have helped the modern marketers? Over 50 years ago when Rich and Jay started Amway, they did not have answering machines, fax machines, PCs, laptops, PDAs, cell phones, email, etc. You may wonder how the early pioneers in MLM ever did their business!

8. Interesting questions we should ask ourselves

Automobiles are now sold on the Internet

How will this affect the car salesman and the landlord who rents out the showroom?

Can insurance also be sold through the Internet?

Jewelry can be bought on the internet, often times eliminating 3-4 middlemen.

How will this affect retail stores that have to carry inventory, security, rent etc?

Can the computer replace engineers?

We have already seen bank tellers replaced by machines.

The internet is driving down real estate broker's fees

With a few mouse clicks, you can see the floor plan, photos of the garden and get a mortgage to buy the property.

Why did IBM spend so much money on a super computer called Deep Blue?

Just to play chess? Think again. At the end of December 1999, IBM announced a $100 million exploratory research initiative, to build a supercomputer 500 times more powerful than the world's fastest. The new computer, nicknamed "Blue Gene" by IBM researchers, will be capable of more than one quadrillion operations per second (one petaflop). This level of performance will make Blue Gene 1,000 times more powerful than the Deep Blue machine that beat world chess champion Garry Kasparov in 1997, and about 2 million times more powerful than today's top desktop PCs.

Why is IBM investing so much money in this type of technology? A technology where, when all the necessary information and data is put into the computer, it can think for itself. I can see a time in the very near future, when it will be possible to have the complete blueprints of a building drawn up by a computer, in seconds, at the push of a button, dispensing with much of the need for architects or engineers, and replaced by someone only needed in order to put in all the required information.

Interior designers will also be replaced very soon by the ability to use a computer to go to on-line sites to shop and choose what we want, from flooring, to wallpaper, to bathroom faucets, and to then change the combinations until we are satisfied with the resulting effect.

A recent program on the Discovery Channel talked about airplanes in the 21st century that will be fully automated and require no pilots. A cockpit

16

where there is a pilot and his dog; the pilot's job just to sit there, and the dog's job to bite him if he touches anything!

By the time this book is ready, much of what I have written about may already be things we take for granted, or regard as old information.

Which professionals cannot be replaced?

Tiger Woods is one. Try to name a few more?

Will your job safety also be affected by technology?

9. Make a decision

Make a decision…
   a) to sow your seeds in your own MLM garden and not to forget the saying, "Do not dig your well only when you need a drink."
   b) to stay focused.
   c) that you cannot fail in MLM.

10. Conclusion

Story: Alexander the Great

Alexander the Great went to war with a country, only to find on arrival that the army of the enemy was three times larger then his. He asked his men and generals to go to the beach, ordered all their ships to be set on fire and then told them they had to fight, as there was no way of going back. He won.

Every distributor must face the fact that because most of them are now living in a developed country, their ship has already been set on fire. Go out now and fight to win, because you cannot lose. You cannot fail in MLM.

Workshop: If you want to start your own business

If you want to start your own business (traditional not MLM), what business will you choose?

_____

_____

_____

What are the requirements, qualifications or challenges you will face for the above-mentioned business? Here are some questions to help you:

How much money do you need for rental down payment?   =

How much money do you need for renovation?   =

How much money do you need for inventory?   =

How much money do you need for advertisement?   =

How many employees and their monthly salary?   =

How much money do you need for unexpected surprises?   =

The most important question

How much money do you have in the bank today?   =

You cannot fail in MLM

Outline for Lesson 1
Why you cannot fail in MLM

1. Introduction

Facts about financial freedom

Job (Just Over Broke) vs Your own business

MLM may be the only vehicle to your dreams

2. People we meet in MLM

a) People who would not even come to a meeting.
b) People who come but have no interest.
c) People who join but never do anything.
d) People who show initial interest but give up easily.

3. Two challenges faced by Multi-Level marketers

The 80% - 20% Rule

We only have ourselves to blame

a) Some companies are not MLM but pyramid schemes.
b) 90% of new MLM companies will not reach their fifth birthday.
c) Many leaders exaggerate.
d) The amount of time we spend criticizing each other.
e) Media reporting which criticizes.

4. The three development stages of a country

Under-developed country

Developing country

Developed country

5. The result in the market place

Big corporations will destroy many small and medium businesses.
"If you can't beat them, join them"

6. On the political front and taxes

Demands for more welfare services and benefits, leading to
correspondingly higher taxes. Well, guess who pays the most taxes?

7. Facts distributors need to face

Little opportunity for traditional business people

It will be difficult to keep up with taxes and inflation

Globalization, the tip of the iceberg

The writing is on the wall.

Is there a bright side?

Several big corporations use MLM.

The growth in MLM

$10 billion in 1980
$40 billion in 1992
$70 billion in 1996
USA MLM statistic 2000:
Combined sales of all MLM = $26 billion out of $3 trillion – hardly 1%
Total annual sales is only Wal-Mart's one month sales
Achievable goal is 3% or about $100 billion for USA.
Worldwide sales for MLM should hit $1 trillion.

Costs of distribution

The high costs of traditional distribution make it possible to sell many things through MLM.

MLM is not really opened yet in the two biggest markets

China and India account for 35% of the world' population.

Story: Many moons

The progress in technology over the last 20 years

8. Interesting questions we should ask ourselves

Automobiles are now sold on the Internet

How will this affect the car salesman and the landlord who rents out the showroom?

Can insurance also be sold through the Internet?

Can the computer replace engineers?

We have already seen bank tellers replaced by machines.

Why did IBM spend so much money on a super computer called Deep Blue?

Just for chess? Think again.

Which professionals cannot be replaced?

Tiger Woods is one. Try to name a few more.

Will your job safety be affected by technology?

9. Make a decision

Sow your seeds in your own MLM garden.
"Do not dig your well only when you need a drink."
Make a decision to stay focused.
Make a decision that you cannot fail in MLM.

10. Conclusion

Story: Alexander the Great

Workshop: If you want to start your own business

Lesson 2
NDO – New Distributor Orientation

1. Purpose

It is very important for all sponsors to teach this exercise to new downline distributors within 48 hours of them joining the business. This is a time when new distributors are excited but generally have no idea of what to do, or even how to approach doing the business. At the same time, there will be a group who are only half-interested, needing another nudge to become committed. It is therefore very important that you help them communicate with themselves, as to their reason for wanting to do the business, and at the same time, lead them into having the right attitude and concept in starting. This will be your first step to success in building a solid downline. I cannot over-emphasize enough, the importance to your organization of producing a great NDO audiotape or CD, so that this training can be given if the upline is too busy. Also, new uplines, still not knowing how to give this training, will then have a tool to help their new downlines, before they have a chance to cool down. A distributor can also turn their car into a classroom.

2. Why did you join the business?

Story: How come you come?

There was an old Chinese man whose name was 'Too old to come'. One day, 'Too old to come' took a new wife who was very young and her name was 'Too young to come'. A year later, they had a baby and they named him, 'How come you come'

So let us begin our NDO by asking all of you, how come you come? Why did you register and join the business in the first place? You may be surprised that over the years, I have heard the following answers:

i) "Ah, ah, ah, ah, I don't know."

ii) "I joined because the sponsor is a close friend and I did not want to offend him/her."

iii) "I joined because my sponsor was very persistent and stayed for hours, so I registered just to get rid of him."

iv) "I only joined so that I can buy the products at wholesale."

v) "I joined because I like the products."

If distributors sign up for any of the above reasons, they will generally not be successful, as they are unclear as to why they got involved in MLM in the first place. Granted, I have heard many stories of successful distributors who first loved the products, and then saw the opportunity. But unless a leader really understands why they themselves are in the business, and what they see in the opportunity, they will not be successful. Let's study some of the reasons why you should get involved and do the business seriously.

3. Reasons why you should get involved in MLM

a) It's a good time to discuss a little about the history of MLM, since you have already decided to be involved in the industry. Way back in the 1920s, a Dr. Carl Rehnborg was working in China and began to observe that the urban Chinese citizens showed signs of malnutrition, but not the poorer citizens living in rural areas. His studies revealed that this was because the richer urban folks were eating polished rice, void in many of the nutrients critical to human diet. After many years of study and research in this field, in 1939 he set up a company called Nutrilite, to manufacture food supplements containing the different vitamins and minerals needed by the body. The major problem he faced was in the marketing and customer education relating to his product range, since most people at that time had not heard about the importance of vitamins and minerals.

To solve the problem, he came up with another new idea in 1945, whereby he used his zealous customers as a sales force, working a system which we today know as Multi-Level Marketing (MLM) or Network Marketing. Under this sales system, distributors sell products, and at the same time are allowed to sponsor other people into the business and be rewarded by way of commissions and other benefits. Dr. Rehnborg deserves recognition as the father of MLM in the history of the industry.

In 1949, two outstanding young men from Grand Rapids, Michigan, had joined Nutrilite and very quickly became the super-stars in the company. Rich DeVos and Jay Van Andel spent 10 years with Nutrilite but in 1959, started a new company called Amway (or American Way), in the basement of their home and the rest, as they say, is history.

From 1945 until the present time, MLM has been laughed at, attacked as a scam, despised and feared by many but has still continued to survive the test of time. It is no longer a new business trend but has proven over the last 50 years or so, to be an excellent channel in the marketing and distribution of goods and services.

This business has exploded over the last 20 years. Way back in 1980 when I first started, the MLM industry worldwide was not even doing US$10 billion, yet by 1992, it was achieving US$40 billion and in 1996, US$70 billion. Looking at that growth between 1980 and 1996, what will the figure be 20 years from now, especially when India and China open up? Just for your information, the population of China is growing at the rate of 60,000 each day, for a net gain of around 16 million people per year. Do we really have to worry about saturation?

b) It is a business that you can choose to be involved in. You can even start part-time, without having to give up your present occupation. It is a fact that many people dare not get involved in traditional business, because it would mean having to give up the job which provides them with the immediate income they need to live on. At the same time, most businesses are not immediately profitable. If you are one of these people, let me invite you to this amazing world of MLM.

c) One of the most exciting things about MLM, is in your ability to leverage and multiply your time through others. I have always considered it as the most important secret to wealth. To be wealthy, you cannot rely on the use of just your own two hands to make money. Here is what I feel sure will be a wake-up story to some of you:

Story: Daddy, how much do you earn per hour?

"Daddy, how much do you earn per hour?" asked the child in a timid voice, when his father came back home from work.

With a harsh tone, the father replied, "Listen son, those are matters that not even your mother knows about. Don't bother me. I am very tired. "But Daddy", the child insisted, "please tell me how much you earn per hour." This time the father's reaction was less harsh and he said, "$20 per hour."

"Daddy, may I please borrow $10?" asked the child. The father became angry and spoke to his son, "So that was the reason why you wanted to know how much I earn. Go to sleep and don't bother me, you selfish child."

During the night, the father was thinking about the incident and started to feel guilty. Maybe his son needed the money to buy something very important. Then, wanting to put his conscience to rest, he went to his son's room and speaking in a low tone, asked his son, "Are you asleep, son?"

"No, Daddy," he responded, half asleep.

"Here's the money that you asked for", said the father. "Thank you Daddy", said the child. At this point, he reached under his pillow and took out some coins. "Now I have enough Daddy. I have $20. Would you sell me one hour of your time?"

If your job pays you on an hourly basis, you will always find it difficult to break away from making ends meet. How much is your time worth?

d) We also hope that this is the place where you can develop your full potential; something many people cannot do, due to lack of opportunity. Maybe this is the only thing available to many of you? Imagine going through life, only working for other people until the day you retire, without ever owning a business that belongs to you. Do not leave this world with your song unsung.

e) Of course we also hope this is the vehicle to help you realize your dreams, but if you think that is too much to ask, you should still consider it as a great source to help you earn supplementary income. Do not go through life financially strapped, especially if you have young children, because they have no control over their lives. Please be responsible. Most families are normally short by only a few hundred or thousand dollars a month, something a good MLM business can easily provide through hard work. These extra hours of hard work, sometimes also take away the extra free time that caused the extra expense, which in turn caused the shortage in the first place.

Story: Jose can you see?

There was a man by the name of Jose, whose dream was to migrate to America. He applied and finally his application was approved.

After arriving, Jose loved everything about America and wrote a lot of letters home, telling everyone how beautiful and prosperous the country was, how friendly Americans were to him, and about all the opportunities available for him to do well.

In one of his letters, he told his friends how nice and friendly everyone was to him. One night, Jose had been invited to a football game, but he did not get a very good seat. 'You know how nice the Americans are to me?' Jose wrote. 'Before the game started, everyone in the stadium stood up and sang in one voice and asked me, "Jose can you see?"
('Oh say can you see?' – the opening verse of the US national anthem)

To all the new people, can you see what we see? If you do, you have taken your first step to success, which means you must have a compelling reason which drives you to want to work hard and pay the price.

4. Be careful when you choose an MLM company

Many people are interested in the multi-level marketing industry, but most do not know how to distinguish between a good company, that will last forever, and one that may be 'just a flash in the pan.'

The failure rate of multi-level companies is exceptionally high because:

a) Inexperienced owners, in not fully understanding the business, design a company that is structured to fail from the word go.

b) Some companies are designed to be 'fly-by-night', playing the 'money game' with the consent and sympathy of distributors, who in turn know that they are involved in a pyramid scheme. They will sometimes even openly boast to prospects, that the company will not last and that everyone must 'hit-and-run.' To companies and people who belong to this group, I have no advice, empathy or need for you. Your type is a 'cancer' to our industry.

5. How to identify a good MLM company

If you are sincerely interested in choosing a good MLM company, we have good news for you. It is one of the easier things to do in this business. Be aware that for a company and you to do well, you need to look at the following requirements:

Products

This is the first thing I want you to look at, when choosing a good MLM company. If a company cannot pass your test of liking the products, then do not even bother to study the marketing plan. In MLM, we are not in the business of selling marketing plans. We sell products. However, many distributors make the mistake of getting excited solely with the compensation, especially with new companies where they are one of the first to join, even though they know the products are garbage. For products, you must consider the following points:

a) Consumable products should be the primary products of any MLM company that is going to last. Ask yourself, if a company does not sell consumable products, can we really talk about a royalty income?

b) All good companies must have a wide range of products, not just a handful. The reason being, that MLM is a business where for you to be successful, you must have a big organization with hundreds or thousands of people. You must have a product range wide enough for these people to choose what they like to sell. They do not need to like everything sold by the company, although we always hope that they will, but we should give them a variety to choose from. For example, if we look at a company selling only cosmetics, you are going to find that the company will normally only have female distributors. However, if you look at the likes of Amway, Forever Living Products, Nu Skin or Herbalife, they have all kinds of distributors, be it male, female, young, middle-aged, old, uneducated, educated, etc.

On top of this, we must never forget that all companies expect their distributors to maintain a fairly good monthly requirement, or the bonuses received will be very small. It is easier to maintain this requirement, when there are many products.

Why then, do some new companies and their leaders, tell their people that the less products the better, and that they should avoid companies with many products? I am sure you may have already clued-in on the answer.

c) Customer satisfaction guarantees not only good products but also ensures that these products are not overpriced, and avoids turning the business into a pyramid scheme. Of course, with a good customer satisfaction guarantee, it is easier to sell products.

d) Good patented products. No company is going to apply for a patent license on a poor product. Additionally, patented products also limit competition.

Company

It is always advisable to look for an established and financially stable company, with a good reputation and background, strong management team and established international markets in place. However, if you come across a new company that interests you, always make sure that the owner of that company is an MLM person, with at least ten successful years of experience 'on the battle front', and not just because they have the money to start an MLM company. I have seen several MLM companies started by billionaires or billion dollar companies, and they are not doing well. Yet it is common knowledge that Rich De Vos and Jay Van Andel started in the basement of their home, with very little money. Never join a company just because the owner is rich. Also never believe them, if they tell you that they employ experts to run the company on their behalf, because that normally results in the employment of 'experts' who are failures in MLM, who do not even have their own organizations, and who are therefore just looking for a pay check. On top of this, many owners will be ego maniacs, not listening to people working for them, even when they themselves do not know what they are doing.

Marketing plan

What is the real bonus paid out by the company?
Is the distribution of bonuses suitable for you and your organization?

This subject will be explored in more detail in Books 2 and 3.

6. Attitude

Commitment

You must make a commitment to do this business for at least one year. All good MLM companies are not 'get-rich-quick schemes' and they are not designed like pyramid schemes, where distributors play the 'money game.' Be careful when you come across companies that tell you there is no need to sell, or that they give you prospects. That all you need to do is to register, and money will start coming in. Do not come with the attitude that you want to be rich in a very short time. We promise you a lot of hard work, but you will have fun and be very proud of the business you are going to build for yourself.

Make a Commitment. Stand in front of a mirror or in front of your spouse and children, and pledge to them that you will take this business seriously and promise to work hard at it for at least one year. Say the following.

I WILL TAKE THIS BUSINESS SERIOUSLY
I WILL COMMIT MYSELF TO LEARN THIS BUSINESS PROPERLY
I WILL WORK HARD IN THIS BUSINESS OF MY OWN FOR AT LEAST ONE YEAR

Have a good learning attitude

Leave behind your past experiences and develop a good learning attitude.

Story: Empty your cup

A young man after becoming very successful, decided to visit his teacher and boast about his success. On arrival, the young man told the teacher that he visited in order to learn more from him, but then began to boast of his own achievements. He then again told the teacher that he wanted to learn more, but before the teacher could say anything, continued to boast of his own achievements and went on and on.

When tea was served, the teacher poured tea into the young man's cup. When the cup was full, the teacher continued to pour until it overflowed. When the tea overflowed, the young man told the teacher, but the teacher continued pouring until the tea overflowed to the floor. The young man told the teacher again that the tea had overflowed.

The teacher then said, "Young man, I cannot teach you anything today, because your cup is already full. Go home and empty your cup, and then come and see me again if you want to learn more."

Over the years, I have seen many highly qualified people join this business, but not become successful because of this mistake. Yes, they may be doctors, lawyers, bankers, and experts in their field, but in MLM, they forgot that they are just kindergarten students.

Believe

Over the years, I have been asked to autograph many things: books, diaries, baseball caps, rally tickets, shirts, napkins, etc., and one word I love to use is, "Believe." It is such an important word in this business:

   a) Company

   If you believe that the company you have joined is not a good one and is out to take you for a ride, how committed will you be?

b) Products

If you believe the company's products are garbage, how good will you be at retailing those products?

c) Yourself

If you do not believe that you can be successful in the business, how hard will you work the business?

d) Uplines

If you believe your uplines are no good and know nothing, how eager are you to ask them to teach and help you?

e) Downlines

Let me share with you something that I have heard several times in over 20 years in the business. I have distributors who tell me that they have sponsored certain individuals, but do not think they will be successful in the business. Isn't this amazing? If they do not believe these downline can be successful, I wonder why they took the trouble to sponsor them in the first place? How eager and willing are they to teach and help them, if they do not believe they can be successful?

Be prepared for discouragement from the following people:

a) People who care about you.

They normally mean no harm, and it may come as a surprise that most times, they try to discourage you, simply because of their care and love for you. They may even think that you have joined some sort of cult or scam, and only be trying to protect you. It can be that they are your elders and still see you as a child, someone who has not yet grown up.

b) Distributors from other MLM companies.

What did you expect?

c) People who are failures themselves.

Story: The hairdresser and the tourist visiting Rome

A tourist one day decided to visit Rome for a holiday, and before the trip, she went to her hairdresser to get a perm. The hairdresser, on learning that she had chosen Rome, began to tell her all the bad things that might happen if she went to Rome.

"Your air ticket will be double-booked," she said, "and on arrival, do not be surprised if your luggage ends up in London, as all airlines going to Rome provide very bad service. Be careful with the taxi driver, for he will probably take you for a ride and try to rip you off," she continued.

She also warned that there would be no guarantees on the hotel reservation, and that the room would probably have been sold to others when she checked in. She then began to talk about how stupid it was and such a waste of time, for tourists to wait at the square on a Sunday, in order to hear the Pope say mass. "All you see is a small figure, wearing a white robe. How do you know it is the real Pope," she asked, "Maybe he is a fake."

The tourist went for her holiday and when she came back, visited the hairdresser again to wash her hair, and the hairdresser began to ask her about her trip.

"Everything happened like you predicted," said the tourist. "My air ticket was double-booked, and because economy and business-class were completely full, I was upgraded to a first-class seat. My luggage, like you said, ended up in London and the airline was very embarrassed, so they gave me $2,000 to buy new clothes. When I got out of the airport, I took a taxi, and the driver drove me all over Rome, because he was new and lost his way. When we finally found the hotel, he did not charge me, and I had seen a lot of Rome for free."

"Like you said, I also had a problem with my hotel reservation; the hotel was fully booked and there was only one room left, the Presidential Suite. Guess where I was sleeping, during my week in Rome? I also made a visit to the square, to see the Pope on Sunday. Do you know that the church has a policy, where the Pope's assistant selects three people every Sunday, and grants them a personal audience with the Pope? I was so lucky, because I was one of the three selected. After the visit, I asked the Pope's assistant why I was selected, and you know what he said?" He said, "Out of so many people, your hair has the worst perm, so I selected you."

It is always amazing, that so many people do not even know how to perm their hair properly, but are always giving their 'expert' and often negative opinion, as to why things cannot be done, and surprisingly, many people listen.

7. Skill

The three "S" for success

Sponsor = 50% of time, but 100% well done.
Sales = 50% of time, but 100% well done.
Service = 100% of time and must be 100% well done.

Success = 200% effort.

Please note their arrangement. Whenever you have a prospect, you must always try and sponsor them first, and then sell products, not vice versa. Yes, there are many distributors who started as customers and later sponsored into the business, but I would not advise you to do your business that way. I have met many distributors who complain that good customers were 'stolen' by other people's downlines. What they fail to comprehend, is that their customers were never their downlines in the first place.

When I was in the restaurant business, I purchased products from several customers of mine, who were involved in MLM. However, none of them were able to get me to attend a business presentation of their opportunity, because their initial approach in selling me products, created a total misconception as to what MLM was all about. Imagine if you were one of those people who failed to sponsor me, because they sold to me first, whereas they should have sponsored me first. Today, my group has sponsored over 2 million distributors. Did anyone really steal me from them, or is it because they themselves failed to sponsor me? Sponsor first, please.

You must have a prospect list (relatives, friends, colleagues, neighbors).

Learn how to invite

Use the telephone when you invite your prospects. Present them with a choice of time and suitable location. Keep the conversation under three minutes, and learn how to hang up the phone.

You must differentiate between invitation and presentation. Be excited and positive. Do not talk about the company, products or the marketing plan, and please, do not feel or act as if you are lying to them. You are just making an appointment to do a presentation.

8. Goal setting

You must immediately set simple, clear and achievable goals. New distributors, already seeing their goals at the initial stage, are normally different from those who just join to 'give the business a try.' In this New Distributor Orientation lesson, you need to learn how to set simple goals, such as how many days in a week they can do the business; how many people they would like to sponsor in a week or a month; how much time they need to have, in order to establish a 10 or 20 customer base; setting some definite dates for the achievement of levels they want to reach on the marketing plan, and how much money they would you like to be making after 3 or 6 months in the business.

Story: The two mental patients

A small mental hospital, due to its limited facilities, has a policy whereby it will give an early discharge to any patient whose case is not very serious. However, before approval is given, all patients have to go through a final interview to satisfy the doctor. Two mental patients, Mr. A and Mr. B, were eligible for discharge, so they went for the final interview with the doctor.

After the interview, Mr. A's discharge was approved but Mr. B was rejected.

Mr. B was very angry and when he met Mr. A, he complained about the matter. Mr. A asked Mr. B, "What question did the doctor ask you?" Mr. B replied, "The doctor asked me what I plan to do, if discharged?" Mr. A said, "I was also asked the same question."

"What was your reply?" asked Mr. B. Mr. A said, "If I'm discharged, I am going to find myself a woman. The doctor said, "That's good, it is normal," so he gave me the discharge."

 "What was your answer?" inquired Mr. A. Mr. B said, "I told the doctor I hate this hospital. In the first place, I am not a lunatic and they made a mistake. During my long stay, I was not treated well, so if and when I am discharged, I am going to buy myself a sling shot, stand outside the hospital and sling rocks to break all the hospital windows."

"You lunatic," said Mr. A. "How can you expect a discharge with such an answer?" So Mr. A taught Mr. B how to answer at his next interview.

Six months later, Mr. B was given a second interview and was asked the same question. He replied, "I am going to get myself a woman", just as Mr. A had taught him. The doctor liked the answer but it just so happened, that the doctor's schedule was quite free that day, so he decided to ask a few more questions.

He asked Mr. B what he was going to do, after he got himself a woman. Now Mr. B, being a bit confused, didn't have an answer. Anyway, digging into his potential, Mr. B replied, "I am going to bring the woman to a room."

"What are you going to do after you bring the woman to the room?" asked the doctor? Mr. B said, "I will then strip the woman naked, take off her bra, and make myself a sling shot..."

Even a madman knows how to set goals!

Today, we are talking about making a decision to get into a business of your own, which is going to be a vehicle to your dreams. For many people, it may be the only vehicle, and to embark on a venture without any set goals, is not the path to success. Put down this book and take 5 minutes to immediately set simple, clear and achievable goals, answering the following few questions:

  a) How many days a week do you want to work the business?
  b) How many people do you want to sponsor, per month?
  c) How many customers do you want to introduce to the products, per month?
  d) How many audiotapes do you want to listen to, per month?
  e) How many times a week will you call your upline?
  f) How many times a week will you call your downlines?
  g) How many days or months do you need in order to hit the first level of success?

9. Responsibility

It is the responsibility of all distributors to maintain their company's suggested retail prices, since price cutting will destroy their market.

10. Opportunity Meeting (Opp.)

You should attend at least five Opp. meetings within a two week period, in order to learn how to present the marketing plan. Bring prospects with you and accompany them throughout the whole meeting. This is one of the most important things to do at this stage, and then make sure you teach the same to all your new distributors - there is nothing more powerful than teaching by example!

By attending and listening to five Opp. meetings within a two week period, you must know how to do a one-to-one Opp.

The **first** Opp. to **excite you**
The **second** Opp. to **learn**
The **third** Opp. to **learn again**
The **fourth** Opp. to **memorize**
The **fifth** Opp. to **internalize**

Golden rules at Opp. meetings

a) Do not leave the meeting while it is still in progress.
b) Refrain from talking to your prospects, as it may disturb the speaker.
c) Help the meeting by supporting the speaker (applaud, laugh or nod in agreement, and do not sit there looking bored or unhappy).
d) Make it your habit to take notes and tape record meetings.
e) Do not bring children. This is a place of business.
f) Turn off or mute all cellular phones or pagers.

11. Sales aids

Make good use of company sales-aids (audiotapes, videotapes, literature, company magazines, etc.). Learn to read the activity schedule of the company or upline, and set your own schedule to attend meetings with your prospects or new downlines. I repeat, read company and upline scheduled activity, and attend the meetings.

12. Tools you need for business

Business cards

Get them printed immediately, as this tool is a must. You can use the ones made by the company, or designed by your group. Normally, this action is also proof that you or your downlines are serious about the business and have not just registered for fun. Do not use the company address or telephone numbers, for two reasons. First, your prospect may show up at the company when you are not there, and as a result, be sponsored by others. Second, no company should have to employ more staff to handle these phones calls.

Start a clear file

It should contain working material about the company and product range, as well as things to help you in your one-to-one OPP. Distributors who start a clear file are really serious about the business, and uplines need to be observant in noticing these small things, in order to locate real leaders in the group. Spend 80% of your time on these people.

A CD or cassette recorder

If you do not own one, you are not in sales. Make it a habit to record all training and speeches, and then to make the recordings available for downlines, if you think they are important or good enough. Always record yourself, and make this a habit. These days, you can also buy recorders with the ability to record up to 6 hours of material, which can then be transferred to your computer, to make very inexpensive CDs.

Know your product line

Start using them.

A pen

This is probably the most important tool we use every day in the business. It is a good idea to reward yourself with a good pen, when you make a good bonus check.

A camera

This equipment is very important, especially when you begin to have downlines. Begin to take photographs of yourself or downlines during meetings and rallies, especially with a guest speaker, high pins and VIPs. If you expect others to take photos for you and then expect to receive them, you will be disappointed. Take responsibility.

An address stamp

With your address and/or telephone number, this will save you a lot of time when you want to give out brochures or flyers.

A computer

Not a necessity, but a good tool in this rapidly changing world.

Proper clothing

Do you really need to buy expensive brand names, to be properly dressed? I don't think so. However, if you are doing well and love expensive clothing, then go ahead, if you want to buy expensive brand names.

Shoes

There is a saying, "If you want to see if a man has style, look at his cloths. If you want to see if a man has money, look at his shoes." Buy good shoes when you are really making good money, to go with your good clothing. I often see people wearing expensive clothing, but wearing shoes that do not go with their clothes.

Makeup

This is a 'must' for all women distributors, as most MLM companies sell health food and beauty products within their product ranges. Men should also use the skin care products sold by their company.

13. Conclusion

There is a price to be paid

Poem:

> The heights by great men reached and kept
> were not attained by sudden flight,
> but they, while their companions slept,
> were toiling upward in the night

Note:

There are three things you must bear in mind:

a) When doing your training, do not try to touch on every point written, since in writing the book, I simply seek to give you a variety of points to choose from.

b) Some points need only be touched upon briefly, since they will be discussed more fully during other training lessons.

c) Tell some of the stories. Do not attempt to tell all of them.

Try and keep the length of the NDO to under two-and-a-half hours.

Outline for Lesson 2
NDO – New Distributor Orientation

1. Purpose

New distributors are excited but have no idea. Teach within 48 hours.
Group who are only half interested and need another nudge.
Teach right attitude and concept when starting.

2. Why did you join the business?

Story: How come you come?

a) Ah, ah, ah, ah, I don't know.
b) I joined because the sponsor is a close friend.
c) I joined because my sponsor was very persistent.
d) I joined so that I can buy the products at wholesale.
e) I joined because I like the products.

3. Reasons why you should get involved in MLM?

a) Proven over the last 50 years to be an excellent channel in the marketing and distribution of goods and services.
b) A business that you can choose to be involved in.
c) Ability to leverage and multiply your time through others.

Story: Daddy, how much do you earn per hour?

d) A place where you can develop your full potential.
e) The vehicle to help you, realize your dreams.

Story: Jose can you see?

4. Be careful when you choose an MLM company

a) Inexperienced owners.
b) Companies that are designed to be fly-by-night companies.

5. How to identify a good MLM company

Products

a) Consumable products.
b) All good companies must have a wide range of products.
c) Customer satisfaction guarantee.
d) Good patented products.

Company

An established and financially stable company.
The owner of the new company is a 10 years MLM person.
Never join a company just because the owner is rich.

Marketing plan

What is the real bonus paid out? Is it suitable for you and your organization?

6. Attitude

Commitment: At least one year.
Have a good learning attitude.

Story: Empty your cup

Believe

a) Company

b) Products

c) Yourself

d) Upline

e) Downlines

Be prepared for discouragement from the following

people

a) People who care about you.
b) Distributors from other MLM companies - what did you expect?
c) People who are failures themselves.

Story: The hairdresser and the tourist visiting

Rome

7. Skill

The three "S" for success

Sponsor = 50% of time, but 100% well done.
Sale = 50% of time, but 100% well done.
Service = 100% of time and must be 100% well done.
Success = 200% effort.

You must have a prospect list (relatives, friends, colleagues, neighbors)

Learn how to invite

8. Goal setting

Story: The two mental patients

Immediately set simple, clear and achievable goals:

a) How many days a week do you want to work the business?

b) How many people do you want to sponsor, per month?

c) How many customers do you want to introduce to the products, per month?

d) How many audiotapes do you want to listen to, per month?

e) How many times a week will you call your upline?

f) How many times a week will you call your downlines?

g) How many days or months do you need, in order to hit the first level of success?

9. Responsibility

It is the responsibility of all distributors to maintain suggested retail prices – price cutting will destroy the market.

10. Opportunity Meeting (Opp.)

You should attend at least five Opp. within a period of two weeks. Do a one-to-one Opp. after two weeks.

11. Sales aids

Read company and upline activity schedule and attend meetings.

12. Tools you need for business

(Keep only to the following)
Business cards - get them printed immediately.
Start a clear file.
A CD or cassette recorder - if you do not own one, you are not in sales.
Know your product line. Start using them.

13. Conclusion

There is a price to be paid

Poem

Lesson 3
Prospecting and Invitation

1. Introduction

After registering with your company, you should begin your business by drawing up a prospect list. There are millions of people who need a secondary income, a change in their occupation, a business opportunity, or perhaps even just something more to do with their lives. But more importantly, even at this early stage of your business, you must realize that for you to be truly successful in MLM, you cannot ignore the wholesale part of your business. It is this part which will reward you with a leadership bonus, considered by many distributors to be the most important stream of income. Sponsoring other people into the business will also help you multiply your time through others, something all successful business people use as a key to great wealth. Remember, that if you help enough other people get what they want, you will always get what you want. Do not go through life just helping yourself; often a cause for regret in people's twilight years.

Sponsoring = Wholesale = Leadership Bonus = Most

important income

2. Your prospect list

Sometimes new distributors feel that they have few or no friends. The section which follows is designed to help you think of people who could be your prospects, and if you spend even just ten minutes on preparing your list, you cannot but help become even more excited about the business.

Your possible prospects (10 minutes)

Family	store owners	travel agent
Club members	Teachers	postman
Bankers	colleagues	classmates
your dentist	neighbors	your hairdresser
church members	Relatives	former office colleagues
your doctor	Friends	people you respect

Now using the above, let us try and take 10 minutes to put together a prospect list of twenty people to get you started. Do not worry if you cannot remember their telephone numbers now. Have fun.

WORKSHOP (10 MINUTES)

Name list of 20 prospects

1. Name_____ Tel. _____ 1st contact_____

   2nd contact_____ Follow up/ remark_____

2. Name_____ Tel. _____ 1st contact_____

   2nd contact_____ Follow up/ remark_____

3. Name_____ Tel. _____ 1st contact_____

   2nd contact_____ Follow up/ remark_____

4. Name_____ Tel. _____ 1st contact_____

   2nd contact_____ Follow up/ remark_____

5. Name_____ Tel. _____ 1st contact_____

   2nd contact_____ Follow up/ remark_____

6. Name_____ Tel. _____ 1st contact_____

2nd contact_____ Follow up/ remark_____

7. Name_____ Tel. _____ 1st contact_____

   2nd contact_____ Follow up/ remark_____

8. Name_____ Tel. _____ 1st contact_____

   2nd contact_____ Follow up/ remark_____

9. Name_____ Tel. _____ 1st contact_____

   2nd contact_____ Follow up/ remark_____

10. Name_____ Tel. _____ 1st contact_____

   2nd contact_____ Follow up/ remark_____

11. Name_____ Tel. _____ 1st contact_____

   2nd contact_____ Follow up/ remark_____

12. Name_____ Tel. _____ 1st contact_____

   2nd contact_____ Follow up/ remark_____

13. Name_____ Tel. _____ 1st contact_____

   2nd contact_____ Follow up/ remark_____

14. Name_____ Tel. _____ 1st contact_____

   2nd contact_____ Follow up/ remark_____

15. Name_____ Tel. _____ 1st contact_____

   2nd contact_____ Follow up/ remark_____

16. Name_____ Tel. _____ 1st contact_____

   2nd contact_____ Follow up/ remark_____

17. Name_____ Tel. _____ 1st contact_____

   2nd contact_____ Follow up/ remark_____

18. Name_____ Tel. _____ 1st contact_____

2nd contact_____ Follow up/ remark_____

19. Name_____ Tel. _____ 1st contact_____

2nd contact_____ Follow up/ remark_____

20. Name_____ Tel. _____ 1st contact_____

2nd contact_____ Follow up/ remark_____

If you find the workshop difficult, then enjoy the story below.

Story: Confession

There was a man who had the habit of having extra-marital affairs, but always regretting it later. He would often go to confession, and one day after an affair, he went to church with a friend to confess his sin. He went inside while his friend waited outside for him.

During the confession, the priest asked him who he had the affair with, but the man pleaded with the priest not to press him for an answer. The priest said, "My son, if you do not tell me, how can I help you?" The man again pleaded with the priest not to press him for an answer, and the priest then said, "I think I know whom you had an affair with. She must be the sister of Mr. Wang" and the man replied, "No, it's not her."

The priest then said, "Then she must be the youngest daughter of Mr. Yang." Again the man said it wasn't Miss Yang either. The priest then guessed that she must be the widow of Mr. Liew, but again the man said it was not she.

"Tell me then who she is," the priest demanded. Again the man pleaded with the priest not to press him for an answer, as he had vowed never to tell anyone the name of the guilty party. At this point, the priest got angry and asked him to leave, and refused to help him with his confession.

The man went outside where his friend was waiting, and the friend asked if he had confessed his sin. The man replied, "No, but let me tell you a piece of good news. I got three new prospects."

So, those of you who think you have no friends, perhaps you should visit your priest tomorrow!

3. The two correct attitudes for invitation

First is your desire to sponsor them because you want to be successful

yourself. This normally is the initial reason, as you understand the law of leverage, and the wholesale part of the business.

Second is even more powerful than the first. It is your sincere desire to

help others, because they need this business. I hope that as you develop into a strong leader, this will become one of your main characteristics.

There are three kinds of love

Give them some thought:
  a) I love you because I want you - humans have this kind of love, as do animals.

  b) I love you because I need you - domestic pets normally give this kind of love, as they need us to feed them.

  c) I love you because you need me - only humans can give this kind of love.

4. You must do the following

  a) Have a prospect list. Make it a habit to keep at least 20 prospects on your list at all times. You should start with the people you know.

  b) Constantly add new names to your list. Have the daily habit of exchanging a name or business card with one or two persons. At the very least, you must exchange a name card with a stranger every week. A good marketer is one who can also sponsor strangers, and remember, a stranger is a friend you have not yet met.

Story: Two Name cards

One day I was listening to a motivational tape about an old lady in the business. She self-proclaimed that she didn't know much about the business, but the one thing she knew she was good at was meeting people. Every day, she would exchange at least two of her name cards with new acquaintances. I took that lesson and I applied it. When I arrived in Taiwan, I didn't have a single lead, so I decided to exchange name cards with at least two new acquaintances a day.

One night, after a long day, I saw a man standing at a bus stop, waiting to go home. I had only changed one name card that day and had one left. It was late and I was exhausted, but I had to keep this promise to myself. I approached the man and I asked to exchange a name card with him. Imagine, it's 11:30pm, and a stranger walks up to you asking to swap name cards. Like many people, he was a bit taken aback and dubious of what my intentions really might have been! I told him, "I am a businessman and it is my goal to exchange name cards with at least two people everyday. I have only exchanged one name card so far today. Please change cards with me, so that I can go home." He did and I went home. In this business, don't try to re-invent the wheel; learn from the experience of others.

    c) Ask for referrals from prospects that are not interested.

    d) Care about people and events around you. If this is your nature, you will never run out of prospects.

5. You must <u>not</u> do the following

a) Do not judge your prospects
   Two major mistakes can be avoided here:

    i) First, is to think that others are not good enough. They are too young, too old, not educated enough, too low in social status, difficult people, etc. I have two leaders I would like to mention, in order to illustrate the point. One was a student, who joined my organization when he was only 20 years old, and after five years in the business, made over US$300,000. Today, he is still in the business full-time, has never looked for a job and wonders why he spent so much time in school. Another leader of mine was a gangster, who after joining, decided to go straight. To date, he has made nearly a million dollars. I feel very lucky to have both of them in my group, and all because their sponsors did not think they were too young or not good enough to join the business.

Remember that in MLM, when you have a successful line, it is an organization of people. Do not be surprised when it happens that your most successful leader in the line, is not the person you personally sponsored, but rather someone under him or her in that organization.

Do not be surprised to find an eagle under a turkey, or a diamond under an idiot.

ii) Second, is to think that others are too good and do not need the business. Perhaps because you see them as already wealthy, famous, too educated, too successful, etc. and therefore assume they will not be interested in the business. It is a fact in life, that people who need money the most, do not know how to make money. Successful people know a good opportunity when they see one.

Story: The electrician

A successful restaurant owner, with the best-located restaurant in a small community, had several customers who were involved in MLM. He bought products from a few of them, and most of them never tried to sponsor him, because they thought he was too busy or too successful, and would therefore not be interested in the business.

Eventually, he was sponsored into the business by one of his customers and became very successful, with an organization of over 100,000 distributors. One day, the former restaurant owner was invited to be a guest speaker at a company rally. After the rally, an electrician who was also a distributor, came forward and hugged the speaker. They knew each other well; because the electrician was a regular at the restaurant and their homes were only about three minutes drive apart. Also, the electrician had been to the speaker's home several times to do repair work. He asked the speaker, "Why didn't you tell me you were interested in the business? I would have sponsored you."

The name of the restaurant owner is yours truly, Eddy Chai, and today my organization has sponsored over two million distributors. Ouch! Having read my book this far, you already know that I started off being very negatively biased against the industry. But if I had not been, and wanted to find a sponsor and MLM company to get involved with, do you think I would walk around with a sign that read, "I am interested in MLM; please sponsor me."?

b) Do not think it is very complicated
Doubt and worries will lead to fear, and fear will lead to inaction. Just do it. I do understand that even simple things, like how to phone a prospect, or turning the cell phone to vibration or mute during meetings, have to be taught to new people. But the fact is, MLM is really quite a simple business. Just do it. Let go of your worries and remain excited.

Story: "Mom, where did I come from?"

A young nine-year-old boy came home from school one day and asked his mother, " Mom, where did I come from?" The mother, not really wanting to deal with 'the birds and the bees' question, decided that her son should ask his dad, since fathers are supposed to have this talk with their son.

When the father came home from work, the boy asked the father where he came from. The father was quite taken aback by the question, but after giving the matter some thought, decided to explain everything to his son. So he began with 'the birds and the bees' and gave a long detailed explanation, and after he had finished, asked the boy why, being so young, he wanted to know.

The boy replied, "Oh, because my friend Tommy told me he came from Chicago."

6. Invitation

A good invitation is making an appointment without going into an explanation of the business. There is a difference between invitation and presentation.

This is a very common misunderstanding with new and inexperienced distributors, as they sometimes feel that if they do not immediately go into the details, they are in some way lying or being misleading to their friends or family.

Over the years, I have heard people from several companies laugh at or put down Amway, because of the curiosity approach their distributors are taught to use, often claiming this as proof that the distributors are not proud of their company. If you believe this nonsense, try to sponsor a committed Amway distributor, and the experience will teach you otherwise. Perhaps my story as to how my first upline in MLM, Calvin, only initially made an appointment but eventually sponsored me, will put an end to this sneering attitude. I would never have given him a chance to talk to me about the business, had he told me it was Amway in the first place. Learn from Amway. They are very good at what they do, and admit your own inexperience. An invitation is different from presentation.

I am aware that most Amway, Forever Living Products, Herbalife, and Nuskin distributors, these days design their own name cards, instead of using the company one, simply because they have become so big and successful, that even using the company name card will spoil their invitation. However, distributors in other Network Marketing companies can use their company designed name card, and still use the curiosity approach. So instead of perhaps laughing at these distributors, why not work hard to make your company just as big and famous, so that you understand the challenges borne out of success? There must be many reasons why Amway are still the biggest and most successful network company, other than the fact that they have been around longer.

Have you ever wondered why it is, that people who we think of as not being as smart or good looking as us, are often more successful and richer than we are? The point here is, that you must 'empty your cup' and be prepared to learn from others. Feel free to try going into details, if you do not believe what I tell you, but also please promise me one thing. If your method does not work, do not just give up the business, because you have not yet learned enough.

The four keys to invitation are courage, enthusiasm, action and belief in success, even before you lift up the phone.

Some stories you may find useful

For courage
Story: The tribal chief and the timid brave

One day, a tribal chief promised the braves of his tribe the hand of his beautiful daughter and half of his land, to the one who would swim across a crocodile infested river and prove himself worthy. Suddenly there was a splash and one brave swam across. He was known as the most timid among the braves and as the chief congratulated him, he kept on looking over his shoulder. The chief was annoyed and asked him why, to which he replied that he would like to find out who had pushed him into the river.

For enthusiasm or taking action

Story: Christopher Columbus

Christopher Columbus was the world's most remarkable salesman. He started out not knowing where he was going. When he got there, he didn't know where he was. When he returned, he didn't know where he had been. He did all this on borrowed money, and managed to get a repeat order.

For belief

Story: A professor from Cornell University

A professor from Cornell University told his story. When he was a student there during the 1930s, he studied very hard, because the best student was promised a job upon graduation. Many times he arrived late to class, because he studied late into the night. On the final exam, he also studied late into the night and overslept. When he arrived, the exam has already started. All the students were given four questions on paper and two questions on the board. He only managed to finish five of the questions and was very depressed, as he knew several students had finished all six.

One early morning, there was a knock on his door and it was his professor, who had come to congratulate him, as the final results were out and he was the top student. He asked the professor why and was told that the exam was on the four questions on the paper, and that the two questions on the board were bonus questions, which Einstein could not solve. He had solved one of the bonus questions, not knowing that they were unsolvable by Einstein!

What do you think might have happened, if he had not been late and had been told that the two questions were ones that Einstein could not solve?

7. How to make an invitation

a) Use the phone.
b) Do not exceed three minutes.
c) Learn how to end the conversation.
d) Do not lie to your prospects.

Here are some examples to give you a feel for what you should do:

Example A

You: Hello! John. I have something exciting that I would like to discuss with you. Is there any chance you will be free, either Monday or Wednesday, so that we can meet and talk? (be *excited*)
John: What is it about? Can you tell me over the phone?
You: It will be impossible for me to explain everything clearly to you over the phone, and I need an hour of your time. Let us spend some time and talk when we meet, if that is ok with you?
Or: It will be impossible for me to explain everything clearly to you over the phone, and I need an hour of your time. Do you have an hour you can give me now? I can drive over to your place and we can talk.
John: Ok! Monday night will be fine.
You: Great, I will wait for you at 7:30pm at the Hyatt. Please be on time.

Example B

Here is a really simple one for very good friends or relatives:
You: Hi Sis, are you doing anything tonight?
Sis: Nothing. Just staying home.
You: Great, because I would like to come over to talk to you about something very important. I will be over after dinner, OK?
Sis: OK.

Example C

This is something I would like you to try if you are new in the business, so that you can learn more about how some of your prospects may feel about the industry. There is nothing like learning from first-hand experience. However, I want you to go into it with a good state of mind. Expect success.

Be open to listening to others and understand that many people have a total misconception about the industry, or may have already had a bad experience with it. Do not argue with your prospects, and remember that they are not stupid and ignorant. I would really like to see your belief level tested and how well your upline has trained you. Have fun and enjoy yourself.

You: Hi Tom, will you and your wife be free on Monday or Tuesday night, as I would like to visit to discuss something important with both of you?
Tom: Is it MLM? Because if it is, I am not interested.
You: Yes it is and I am glad you tell me you are not interested, because I have just got involved. Tom, will you do something for me? I would like your advice, to help me see if I should be involved in this business. As you must have some experience you can share with me, can you do this for me?
Tom: Sure. Come over after dinner.
You: Thanks Tom. Appreciate it. I will be over at 8.00pm.

Do not lie to your prospects and when you go to see them, do not try and force the business on them. Your job is to show them the business and they can make their own intelligent decision. That's it.

Example D

With many companies, distributors are able to expand their business overseas into other international markets, so I must also do an example of an invitation in this area.

You: Hello, can I speak to Mr. Singh please?
Mr. Singh: Speaking.
You: Hi Mr. Singh. My name is Mr. Smith. We met on the plane two days ago, when I was coming to your country. Do you remember me?
Mr. Singh: Of course I do. How are you Mr. Smith? Are you enjoying your stay here?
You: Yes I am. Mumbai is certainly a big place. (After all the small talk.) Mr. Singh, the reason I am calling, is because I have come to India to start a new business venture. There is a possibility that we can do something

together. Can we meet to talk about it?

Mr. Singh: Sure. (If Mr. Singh asks about the business, go to Example A)

You: Great. I am staying at the Taj Mahal Hotel. Can we meet at the coffee shop on the first floor? What time will be convenient for you?

Mr. Singh: 2.00pm will be fine.

You: Great. I will see you then. Bye.

8. Be prepared for certain situations and use some common sense

a) Traffic jam. Your prospect can be late. You cannot.
b) Be clear about coming for dinner, or after dinner.
c) Give yourself enough time between appointments.
d) Make sure the prospect is free and respect their time.
e) Use your common sense, although I do understand that sometimes common sense is not that common. To talk to a prospect who owns a restaurant during lunch or dinner times, is not a good idea.
f) Know your prospects. If they do not like to come out, go to their home.
g) Polish your telephone skills.

9. F.O.R.M.

F.O.R.M. stands for:

F = Family
O = Occupation
R = Recreation
M = Message

When you meet new prospects and you do not know them, listen to their needs by using F.O.R.M. Listen to your prospects when they talk about their family, occupation and recreation. From this, you will get the message, or their needs, and normally be able to figure out where your business will be able to satisfy their needs. Do not behave as if you are a policeman interrogating a criminal.

Example E

You attended a wedding dinner and were sitting beside a couple, about to migrate to Canada. During the conversation, they may tell you that they are looking for something to do when they migrate. Let them do the talking and just listen to their F.O.R.M. When you phone them, you already know their needs.

You: Hi Mr. Lee. I am Mr. Smith. We met last week at Susan's wedding. Do you remember me?
Mr. Lee: Hi Mr. Smith. Of course I remember you. How nice of you to call.
You: Mr. Lee. You were telling me that when you migrate to Canada, you are looking for something to do. The reason I'm calling, is that my company also has an operation there, and maybe there is a chance we can do something together. Can we get together some time this week, say Monday or Tuesday, to discuss this?
Mr. Lee: Sure.
You: Great. Let's meet on Monday at 2.00pm at the Hyatt, and we will take it from there. See you then. Bye.

10. Conclusion

Do not let anyone steal your dreams. As a salesperson, remember not everything is a 'bed of roses', and just because you are excited and see your dreams becoming a reality in this business, let me warn you that there will be people who think you are crazy, brain-washed, and have joined a cult. I have got good news for you. Most people thought Columbus was crazy too, so let's end this lesson with a story:

Story: Let the dogs bark but the caravans move on

In the olden days, traders would conduct their trade in caravans, and when they got ready to leave their village in the early morning, they would wake up the dogs, and these dogs would bark and create a lot of commotion. Eventually, these caravans would be ready and move out of the village and be on their way to work.

So when people laugh at you, put you down, discourage you, reject you, slam the door on you, I want you to remember, "Let the dogs bark but the caravans move on."

Good luck. Have a happy journey. My heart and thoughts will be with you. Let's get to work.

Outline for Lesson 3
Prospecting and Invitation

1. Introduction

Sponsoring = Wholesale = Leadership Bonus = Most

important income

2. Your prospect list

WORKSHOP (10 MINUTES)

Name list of 20 prospects

Story: Confession

3. The two correct attitudes for invitation

a) First is your desire to sponsor them because you want to be successful.
b) Second is your sincere desire to help others.

Three kinds of love

a) I want you.
b) I need you.
c) You need me.

4. You must do the following

a) Have a prospect list.
b) Constantly add new names to your list.

Story: Bend the wiper

c) Ask for referrals from prospects that are not interested.
d) Care about people and events around you.

5. You must <u>not</u> do the following

a) Do not judge your prospects
   i) First is to think others are not good enough.
   ii) Second is to think that others are too good.

Story: The electrician

b) Do not think it is very complicated. Doubt = Worries = Fear = Inaction

Story: "Mom, where did I come from?"

6. Invitation

An invitation is different from presentation

The four keys to invitation:
   courage
   enthusiasm
   action
   belief in success, even before you lift up the phone

Some stories you may find useful

For courage: The tribal chief and the timid brave

For enthusiasm or taking action: Christopher Columbus

For belief: A professor from Cornell University

7. How to make an invitation

a) Use the phone.

b) Do not exceed three minutes.

c) Learn how to end the conversation.

d) Do not lie to your prospects.

Examples

8. Be prepared for situations and use some common sense

a) Traffic jam. Your prospect can be late. You cannot.
b) Be clear about coming for dinner or after dinner.
c) Give yourself enough time between appointments.
d) Make sure the prospect is free and respect their time.
e) Use your common sense. To talk to a prospect who owns a restaurant during lunch or dinner hour is not a good idea.
f) Know your prospects. If they do not like to come out, go to their home.
g) Polish up your telephone skills.

9. F.O.R.M.

F = Family
O = Occupation
R = Recreation
M = Message

Use FORM to listen to their needs

Do not behave as if you are a policeman interrogating a criminal.

Example

10. Conclusion

Story: Let the dogs bark but the caravans move on

Lesson 4
The Importance of Image
1. Introduction

You need not be a businessperson to join this business, but you must understand that MLM is a business, so after joining, you should act as a businessperson and have the image of one. If need be, change your identity to fit the new role that you want to play. You are now in a business of your own, the President of your own company and a leader of your organization.

Can a monk who joins the police force refuse to put on his police uniform, because he still prefers his robes? Or a policeman who leaves the force to become a monk, refuse to put on his robes, because he prefers the uniform of policeman?

Story: Lady coming home, one late, rainy night

A young lady coming home very late, one rainy night, saw a stranger standing outside the gates of her apartment building. The street was deserted and the man was dressed in very shabby clothes, wearing a pair of dark sunglasses, with long hair down to his shoulders.

If you were that young woman, how would you feel?

If you're afraid, why do you feel this way? Could it be possible that the man of whom you are afraid, is a very good, God-fearing man, a great father and husband, or maybe even a very famous artist? Heck, it may even be Tom Cruise in person!

A young lady coming home very late, one rainy night, saw a stranger standing outside the gates of her apartment building. The street was deserted and the man was dressed in a policeman's uniform.

If you were that young woman, how would you feel?

If you are not afraid, why do you feel this way? Is it not possible, that this man is a very dangerous criminal who has just killed a policeman, and that everything he is wearing is from the dead policeman?

Is it not possible, that the first man is an undercover agent and the real policeman, while the second man is one of the most wanted men in the country?

Image is so important, as it is common for people to stereotype others, without even knowing who they are. New prospects, not knowing who or what you are, may judge you and your business by your image, and may not give you a second chance.

Story: Job interview

You go for a job interview in a dirty old office, where the boss offers you a high wage, and then go for another interview in a beautiful, clean, well-decorated office, where the boss offers you a lower wage. Which will you choose?

I think most of you will choose the second.

2. Image has four areas: Inner, Outer, Company and Product

a) Inner image
   i) Finding yourself a role model is the easiest route by which you can learn.
   ii) Make a decision that you want to be a positive, optimistic, enthusiastic, and exciting person. Remember, being negative, unhappy, filled with doubt and no courage, is also a decision you

have made for yourself.

iii) Form good habits: read at least one book per month, listen to one audio tape a week, and record and take notes when listening to trainings or rallies. Always ask yourself what you have learnt from them, and take immediate action to improve your identity. One of the most valuable things I learnt from the great master Anthony Robbins, is that you can always recreate your identity, and this lasting change can be done in a heartbeat. Buy all books and tapes by this great master when you come across them, and it will be money well spent.

1. Many people never make any effort to learn.
2. Some learn, but do not understand what they have learnt.
3. Some learn, understand what they have learnt, but do not do what they have learnt.
4. Some learn, understand what they have learnt, and do what they have learnt.

Make your decision.

iv) Develop a sense of humor and learn to laugh at yourself.

v) It may surprise you to know, that looking at someone's eyes during a conversation, giving a firm handshake, and walking straight and upright without slouching, are all part of an inner image.

vi) Take the initiative to start a conversation, smile and be happy.

b) Outer image

i) What you wear, and how you look after your outer image, can affect your confidence and behavior, and also tells a lot about whether you like yourself or not. People who know how to look after themselves, love themselves in a nice way!

ii) Be a product of your products. The majority of MLM companies have health and beauty products as at least part of their product range, so take care of your hairstyle, weight, teeth, skin, etc. Use the products sold by your company and never use another brand of similar product, unless you have a very good reason, maybe due to allergies.

iii) Know pleasing color combinations.

1. Have you heard people say, you look so young today?
2. Have you heard people say, you look so beautiful today?
3. Have you sometimes looked at a person in a crowd, and he or she just stands out?
4. Do you have your favorite dress - favorite tie?
5. Have you heard people ask you, whether you are feeling well today?
6. Have you said to yourself, you have no clothes to wear, even though you have a closet full of them?

If you answer, "yes" to the above, I would like to recommend two books: "Color me beautiful" by Carole Jackson or "Your new image" by Gerrie Pinckney and Marge Swenson.

iv) Dress properly for the occasion.
1. For parties and formal occasions.
2. When conducting business meetings, training or attending rallies.
3. During leisure time or days off, I will still advise you to look after your image.
4. Be neat and clean, because you may not know whom you may be meeting - he or she may be your best prospect.

v) Your family image, as seen by your associates. Do you have a happy family? Never make the mistake of quarrelling or putting down your spouse or partner in front of your downlines. Remember, your spouse or partner is also their upline!

vi) When using your home for home parties or meetings, make sure your home is neat and clean.

vii) Keep your vehicle clean, inside and out. You may need it to transport your prospects or downlines to meetings and rallies. I heard a financial expert, who said that people with dirty cars, are normally people who owe money on their credit card. A car is probably your second most expensive purchase, next to your house, and if you do not even know how to keep it clean, you may be displaying the character or a person who does not know how to look after things which are important to them.

c) Company image
i) Be a leader who is happy, excited and likes to share with others

when participating in company events and meetings. Go around shaking hands and welcoming new people to the event, especially if you are a high pin leader. Do not just sit in the front row, waiting for downlines to bring people to you. Walk around. It is good for your leg muscles!

ii) Help keep all meeting venues clean, especially venues you rent from others. There are three kinds of people:

1. Those who have a habit of throwing rubbish and thinking it is all right to do so.
2. Those who throw rubbish into rubbish bins, or keep it until they find a bin, because they believe that throwing it anywhere else is wrong.
3. Those who will only throw rubbish into rubbish bins, and will also pick up rubbish thrown away by others.

Decide what kind of person you want to be, because at age 65, your bank account will probably reflect to which of the three categories you belong. People who do not know how to look after others, the country and society, normally have no money, while people who only know how to look after themselves, may have some money. On the other hand, people who know how to look after others, themselves, the country and society, often become wealthy. If you have room for improvement, decide and recreate your new identity now!

iii) Participate in social activities with your group. For example, donate old toys, old clothing, help clean the beaches and parks, do some work in your local hospital, the home for the aged, the orphanage, protect the environment, etc.

iv) When holding home parties or meetings, be considerate of your neighbors. Even though you are working from home, you still represent your company to them, so show consideration, for example, by controlling noise levels and making sure that their driveways are not blocked with vehicles.

d) Product image
   i) Do not cut prices.
   ii) Do not exaggerate.
   iii) Use your products and be proud of them.

3. Conclusion:

Story: A professor did a study on image at a train station

First, he dressed up as a beggar, and asked people to give him some money for his train fare, because his wallet had been stolen. He collected only US$32.

Next, he cleaned up and dressed as a professor. He stood at the same spot in the train station, and told passersby that he was a professor, his wallet had been stolen, and he asked them to give him some money for his train fare. He nearly decided to change professions when he collected US$674.

IMAGE TESTING CHART

	Always	Most Times	Rarely
1. I'm about the right weight for my height	5	3	1
2. I look vital and alive	5	3	1
3. I am committed to regular exercise	5	3	1
4. My hairstyle is the right length and well-groomed	5	3	1
5. My fingernails are manicured and hands clean	5	3	1
6. My teeth are polished and well looked after	5	3	1
7. My dress is appropriate for me in each situation	5	3	1
8. The jewelry I wear is suitable for the occasion	5	3	1
9. I look neat and tidy	5	3	1
10. Generally speaking, I am sure my image is good	5	3	1

TOTAL SCORE _____

If you scored above 40, then you probably feel as good as you look. A score between 25 and 40, means that just a little effort is necessary to get yourself up to scratch.

Under 25, means that you really must get serious about how you look. Right now you should set some goals to improve your appearance, and then concentrate on achieving them.

THE E-C FACTORS - ENTHUSIASM AND COMMITMENT, ARE THE KEY FACTORS IN MARKETING YOURSELF AND YOUR TALENTS SUCCESSFULLY TO ANYBODY. YOU NEVER GET A SECOND CHANCE AT CREATING A GOOD FIRST IMPRESSION.

Outline for Lesson 4
The Importance of Image

1. Introduction

MLM is a business. You should act and look like one.

Story: Lady coming home, one late, rainy night

Story: Job interview

2. Image is divided into four areas

a) Inner image
   i) Finding yourself a role model is the easiest route by which you can learn.
   ii) Make a decision you want to be a positive.
   iii) Form good habits. Books, audio tape, trainings, rallies and take notes.
   iv) Develop a sense of humor and learn to laugh at yourself.
   v) Look at people's eyes during the conversation; give a firm handshake.
   vi) Take the initiative to start a conversation; smile and be happy.

b) Outer image
   i) People who know how to look after themselves, love themselves.
   ii) Be a product of your products.
   iii) Know pleasing color combinations.
   iv) Dress properly for the occasion.
   v) Your family image as seen by your associates.

    vi) Your home must be neat and clean for home parties or meetings.

    vii) Keep your vehicle clean inside and out.

c) Company image

    i) Be a leader when participating in company events and meetings.

    ii) Help keep all our meeting venues clean, especially venues you rent.

    iii) Participate in social activities with your group.

    iv) Be considerate of your neighbors.

d) Product image

    i) Do not cut prices.

    ii) Do not exaggerate.

    iii) Use your products and be proud of them.

3. Conclusion

Story. A professor did a study on image at a train station

Workshop: IMAGE TESTING CHART

Lesson 5
How to sponsor

1. Introduction

There are four important secrets to success in MLM. First is sponsor. Second is sponsor. Third is sponsor. Fourth, I forget what it is! Let us not go around in circles, looking for the secrets of success in this business. You become successful and wealthy, because of your ability to form a big organization and maintain it. You can be a great speaker, a great leader, a great person, excited and motivated, but unless you put in the time and effort in sponsoring and help your downlines in sponsoring, you will just be ordinary. I always like to tell distributors, that sponsoring is like putting in golf. You can hit a great straight putt, but if you hit the putt short, it will never go into the hole. So for sponsoring, I would like to remind you to make enough effort. You must hit enough or even if it is not straight, you must hit past the hole.

2. There are several ways of doing business to market goods and services

Let us look at some Marketing Strategies

a) You go to a party, dressed up to look very rich. You hope all the gorgeous girls at the party will come to you and say, "You are very rich. Marry me."

That's Traditional Business

b) You see a gorgeous girl at a party. You go up to her and get her telephone number or email. The next day you contact her and say, "Hi, I'm very rich. Marry me."

That's Telemarketing or Internet Marketing

c) You see a gorgeous girl at a party. You go up to her and say,
"I am very rich. Marry me!"

That's Direct Selling

d) You're at a party with a bunch of friends and see a gorgeous girl.
A couple of your friends corner her, point at you and say,
"He's very rich. Marry him."

That's Multi-Level Marketing

Conventional or traditional business, where you set up shop and wait for customers to come through your door, or if they do not come, then wait to go under. These are opportunities for people who can afford them.

Mail Order, Telephone and Internet Marketing, where an entrepreneur finds a good product and sells it through these channels. Again these are businesses reserved for people who have the means.

Direct Selling, like Avon or Electrolux, where an entrepreneur finds a good product, and employs sales people to go door-to-door, selling the product. This system is good if you own the business. You leverage your time through your sales force, but if you are not the boss, then you are just the sales person, and there is not much difference between you and your **J**ust **O**ver **B**roke employees. You work eight to ten hours a day, five or six days a week, just like a regular job. Do not expect to do very well, as you cannot leverage your time.

MLM. One of the main reasons why so many very highly qualified people are now choosing to be involved in MLM, is because it offers two kinds of business opportunity; a personal retail business, and a wholesale business. To be able to sell products offered by your company is very exciting in its own right, but to then also be able to wholesale products, by sponsoring others into the business, makes this into a really outstanding business. This is especially so, if your company is open in other international markets, where your downlines in other countries are also your wholesale business.

We are now talking about a business with no boundaries, and where the 'sky is the limit' as to how big your business can be. I know of several companies with a presence in over fifty countries, and a few who are into over a hundred. What is the use of having a wholesale business, which comes about because of sponsoring, if you do not do it? If you are given the richest gold deposit in the world, but you make no effort to dig, the gold remains in the ground!

The lifeblood of any MLM business is people, and people come as a result of sponsoring or networking. It is also interesting to note, that networking is also used in religions, and taking Christianity as an example, we are told that Jesus sponsored just 12 disciples, yet today there are estimated to be over 1 billion members! Another interesting thing to note, is that those disciples were instructed to go out two-at-a-time to spread the word, so it would seem that use of the 'ABC method' was started 2000 years ago, but we will cover this topic later.

Franchise businesses, like 7-11, McDonald's, Wendy's, Starbucks, etc., all use networking, as successful business people understand the use of leverage as the most profitable and effective way of doing business.

3. Let us study the law of leverage

If you work 8 hours a day, 5 days a week and there are 4 weeks in a month, you will have:

8hrs x 5 days = 40hrs x 4 weeks = 160 hours per month.

If you get paid:

US$10	x 160 =	**US$1,600 per month**
US$20	x 160 =	**US$3,200 per month**
US$30	x 160 =	**US$4,800 per month**
US$40	x 160 =	**US$6,400 per month**
US$50	x 160 =	**US$8,000 per month**
US$100	x 160 =	**US$16,000 per month**

Let us say, in your country you average about US$20 per hour (I know this is considered too high in many countries) and work 40 hours per week x 50 weeks per year; this will equal 2,000 hours per year and 2,000 hours x US$ 20 per hour = US$40,000 in annual income.

If your break off line makes you US$1,000 per month

If you show your business to your prospects and they become successful, and this line brings you US$1,000 per month in extra income, the chart below will show you how you have leveraged yourself; if you divide the annual income by the average US$20 per hour.

1 x OPP x 2hr = 0 (not interested in the business)

1 x OPP x 2hr = 1 Leader = US$1,000 per month x 12 months = US$ 12,000 / by US$20 per hour = 600 hours per year.

600hours + 2,000 hours you work in your full time job = 2,600 hours per year. A 30% increase.

You have now leveraged yourself an _extra_ 600 hours for the year!

If your break off line makes you US$3,000 per month

What if you found a great leader, and this line gave you an extra income of US$3,000 per month?

1 x OPP x 2hr = 1 great Leader = US$3,000 per month x 12 = US$36,000 / by US$20 per hour = 1,800 hours per year.

1,800hours + 2,000 hours you work in your full time job = 3,800 hours per year. A 90% increase.

This is like working two full time jobs!

If your break off line makes you US$10,000 per month

What if you sponsored a super star, and this line gave you an average income of US$10,000 per month?

1 x OPP x 2hr = 1 super Leader = US$10,000 per month x 12 = US$120,000 / by US$20 per hour = 6,000 hours.

When you divide these 6,000 hours by the average 2,000 hours per year you work in your job, this will equal 3 years.

You have added 3 more working years to your life for every year.

4. The three "S" main foundation to success in MLM

Sponsor = 50% of time, but 100% well done
Sell = 50% of time, but 100% well done
Service = 100% of time and must be 100% well done
Success = 200% effort

Note that I put sponsor first at 50% of your time, and then selling for the remaining 50%, but that does not mean that retailing is unimportant; it is very, very important. MLM is a business where you need lots of people and all distributors must have the responsibility and do their share of retailing, by looking after 10 to 20 customers every month. If you do not like the idea of retailing, I have got good news for you; go out and sell anyway!

5. Who are your prospects?

a) Yourself

Before you sponsor anyone else, please sponsor yourself first. Ask yourself the following questions:

i) Why did you join MLM? Do you believe in our spirit and the concept of the way we do business? You should, if you have not joined a pyramid scheme

ii) Why did you choose your company? Make an effort to understand your company, the products and the marketing plan. Use the products personally. Do you believe in them? Are they fairly priced?

iii) Is it a company you are willing to be committed to, or are you one of the MLM fleas that jump from one company to another, and this is just another stepping stone before the next? Unless you have already sponsored yourself, how powerful will you be when you talk to others?

b) Others

OK, you are now ready to sponsor others, and they are everyone who has reached the minimum age, as required by your company policy.

These people are divided into:

People who have never previously done MLM

These are the people I like the best, as sometimes they are so excited and fearless, they motivate me. Influence them with your excitement, and lead them without taking for granted that they should know even the simple things about MLM.

Those who were involved in MLM before

Learn to analyze and measure their experience in the business. You are going to find all kinds of people here:

i) Those who may have had a previous bad experience with the business, and are now quite negative about it. Do not give up on them if you are now introducing them to a good MLM company. They were interested in MLM before, and will be interested again, probably for the same reasons. The majority of them got burnt, because they joined a pyramid scheme or their company went bust.

ii) Those who were in the business before, and are waiting for a new company to find them! There are many of these people in a mature market, and I also come across many who tell me how much they miss the business and all the good things associated with it; the trainings, the rallies, the recognition, the love and friendship in the group, etc. Finding these people, is like finding a lost brother or sister.

iii) Distributors from pyramid schemes, who bring their unhealthy attitude with them. I am always worried about this group, as we all know it is not easy to 'change the spots on a leopard.' If you are still representing a pyramid scheme, please stop your nonsense.

iv) The so-called leaders, who think they are very good in the business, simply because they were lucky to find a strong leader in one company, and end up with a good group. Most of the time, they are not even on good terms with the real leader who did the work.

v) The ones who tell you they have ten years previous experience, who hardly do the business, but simply joined ten years ago. I hope people who claim to have ten years experience, talk, behave and have the knowledge of leaders who actually have ten years experience. I have to tell you that I measure you by the amount of knowledge you possess, not by the number of years you have been involved.

People from other companies

i) Those who are still actively involved in the business. Do not compare your company with theirs, and do not waste time listening to them about their companies if they have no interest in being sponsored by you, but are really trying to sponsor you instead. Don't fight.

ii) The uplines of the above. Be careful of this group, because they may behave like the mother hen protecting her chicks - they will bite you! Be clear to state your position, and confirm their motives for coming in the first place. Did they come to hear about your company because they are personally interested, or just to protect their downlines? Ask them for the chance to do a proper presentation without any interruption, making it clear that you will answer any questions they may have, after you are finished. Try to understand their state of mind, as you will probably feel the same if someone from another company tries to sponsor your downline. Never end up arguing in front of the prospect, as the upline and the prospect may have a better and longer relationship than yours.

6. Speed of sponsoring

I cannot over-emphasize enough, the importance of sponsoring quickly, and understanding the power of working just a little harder. Understand the power of one. Let me warn you from the outset, that most of the people who fail in MLM do so, not because they do too much, but because they do too little. At the same time, you have to be aware of the differing standards by which we all evaluate ourselves. Over the years, I have come across many distributors who believe they are working very hard according to their standard, but who, according to the standards of very high achievers, may only be ordinary, or even below par. When the tortoise and the hare are having a race, the tortoise may think the hare is just too fast, but when a snail sits on a tortoise, it may be think that it is driving a Ferrari! How do you know you are working hard enough? When you are satisfied with your bonus checks, you are working hard enough.

The power of one

2 x 2	=	4 x 2	=	8 x 2	=	16 x 2	=	32 x 2	=	**64 people**
3 x 3	=	9 x 3	=	27 x 3	=	81 x 3	=	243 x 3	=	**729 people**
4 x 4	=	16 x 4	=	64 x 4	=	256 x 4	=	1,024 x 4	=	**4,096 people**

729 - 64 = 665 people (The real difference is the power of one, where all active distributors are sponsoring 3 new people a month, instead of 2)

4096 - 729 = 3,367 people (The real difference is the power of one, where all active distributors are sponsoring 4 new people a month, instead of 3)

4096 - 64 = 4,032 people (The real difference is two, where all active distributors are sponsoring 4 new people a month, instead of 2)

Theoretically, if every leader has a sales volume of only US$1,000, the result will be the following. Remember, the bottom is just theory. If anyone tells you that this is the way bonuses will be paid, because their company pays up to five or six levels, then you are listening to a bunch of BS and I hope you are not stupid enough to believe such nonsense.

64 x US$1,000 sales	= US$64,000 x 2% bonus	= **US$1,280**
729 x US$1,000 sales	= US$729,000 x 2% bonus	= **US$14,580**
4,096 x US$1,000 sales	= US$4,096,000 x 2% bonus	= **US$81,920**

Story: Tiger Woods Vs. Paul Azinger

Let us look at the small differences in some statistics between a great golfer, Tiger Woods, and another great player, Paul Azinger, for the year 1999, and how these slight differences makes such a great difference between their incomes. Then you may understand why I ask you to train your organization to push themselves a little harder, if they want to do well and make great incomes.

For the average 18 holes, Woods plays 69.56 vs. 71.49 for Azinger.
For putting, Woods averages 29.25 vs. 29.51 for Azinger.
For tee-off distance, Woods averages 293 yards vs. 273 yards for Azinger.
However, the difference in income is US$6 million for Woods vs. US$500,000 for Azinger.

7. The 5 lines 5 leaders system

Beside speed, I want to remind you to sponsor wide and deep. Use the five lines method that I have been using for the last twenty years; that is, to have five active front lines. Work on these 5 lines and at the same time, find at least 5 leaders from these lines, so that when you achieve your first leadership level in your company's marketing plan, you have these 5 leaders. These 5 leaders need not be in 5 separate lines. Normally they will be in 2 or 3 lines, with the other lines having no leader at all, and that is all right. To make your leadership level without any leaders at all, will not give you a healthy organization, but when you make that level and have 5 leaders in the organization, you will soon have leadership lines breaking off under you, and begin to make your royalty income. You must also check that every one of your break-off leaders, have at least 5 leaders in their organization. When your leaders break off as leadership lines, you must find new lines to replace them, so that you keep on growing. Do not put all your hopes and dreams on just one or two lines. If you do not work with five lines, you are not working hard enough. Finally, do not forget to teach your leaders to duplicate this system. When your 5 leaders each have 5 leaders under them, you will have a business built on solid rock.

8. Points to note

a) Use the ABC method. 'A' must know 'C's' F.O.R.M., obtained from 'B'. This will be covered in the next chapter.

b) Learn how to do the one-to-one OPP. Listen to at least five OPPs with prospects.

c) Start organizing home meetings and parties.

d) Be prepared: have company literature, audio videotapes and products on hand.

e) Learn how to answer objections. Be confident, courageous and humble. You must constantly make progress and improve yourself.

f) Have the good habit of sponsoring four people a week when you are new in the business; after all, you have very little work load when your organization is still small.

9. After an OPP., there will be two kinds of prospects

Those who want to join the business

a) Help them to register.

b) Provide a schedule of meetings to attend.

c) Provide audio, videotapes and literature.

d) Teach them how to start a prospect list.

e) Prepare them for discouragement.

Those who are still undecided

a) Try and find out why they are hesitant to join. Answer their objections. The normal ones will be: pyramid scheme, no time, no talent, no friends, no money, no interest, market saturated, etc.

a) Give them follow-up material e.g. audio tapes and/or video tapes, and set an appointment for your next visit.

b) Encourage them, by showing your commitment to help if they want to join.

c) Provide them with exciting news when the opportunity arises. For example, when the President of your company is visiting, there is a rally, new product launch or opening of new markets.

10. Conclusion

There is something you must never do. That is, to give up the business just because some of your prospects, or people very dear to you, do not join your business. It is normal for prospects not to be interested in the business, and sometimes, it is not that they won't join the business, but that they are not yet ready. It took my wife Grace and I, eight years to sponsor her very close friend Stella. She joined after she got married and today is one of our biggest lines, with over half-a-million distributors, a quarter of my business. Also remember, that you must make a commitment to do the business for at least one year.

Story: The Principle of "Next"

When a surgeon operates on a patient and the patient dies, do you think the doctor says, "Aah, the patient is dead. I quit?"

Of course not! What they do is to push the dead person through the back door, and the nurse then goes to the front door and asks, "Next", for the next patient to come to the operating table.

It is not my style to teach people to go out expecting failure, but you must be prepared for rejection, and when your prospect turns you down, do not forget, 'Next". Do not let rejection affect your work and belief levels. It is a fact that the reason I have become so big, is because the number of people who have rejected me, is bigger than the organization of most high pin distributors.

"I've missed more than 9,000 shots in my career. I've lost almost 300 games. 26 times I've been trusted to take the game winning shot and missed. I've failed over and over and over again in my life—and that is why I succeed." ---Michael Jordan

Workshop on sponsoring

Play 1

Select one person to come on stage. They then invite a partner to join them on stage. The two of them, then each invite a partner to come on stage, and so on, and so on. You will immediately see how quickly you fill up the stage.

You will have the same effect, if you teach all your downlines to sponsor one person a month. Let us see the power of leverage. Suppose in the first month, you sponsored one new friend. You then sponsor another one the second month, and your friend sponsor also sponsors one new person. That brings your total organization to four people.

On the 3rd month, your organization will have   8 people

    4th month, your organization will have   16 people

    5th month, your organization will have   32 people

    6th month, your organization will have   64 people

    7th month, your organization will have   128 people

Play 2

Two persons bet on a game of golf and the bet is $1 per hole, doubling the bet for every hole. It so happens that gentleman 'A' lost all the 18 holes to gentleman 'B'. Let us see how much gentleman 'A' will owe to gentleman 'B' at the end of the day.

hole # 1	=	$1
hole # 2	=	$2
hole # 3	=	$4
hole # 4	=	$8
hole # 5	=	$16
hole # 6	=	$32
hole # 7	=	$64
hole # 8	=	$128
hole # 9	=	$256
hole #10	=	--------
hole #11	=	--------
hole #12	=	--------
hole #13	=	--------
hole #14	=	--------
hole #15	=	--------
hole #16	=	--------
hole #17	=	--------
hole #18	=	--------

Quote: Apple seed

Any fool can count how many seeds there are in an apple but who can count how many apples there are in one seed?

Confucius

Quote: 1% vs. 100%

"I would rather have 1% of the efforts of 100 people than 100% of my own efforts."

Paul Getty

Outline for Lesson 5
How to sponsor

1. Introduction

    a) Four important secrets to success in MLM. Sponsor, Sponsor, Sponsor, Sponsor.

    b) Successful and wealthy because of a big organization and maintaining it.

    c) You to make enough effort.

2. Ways of doing business to market goods and services

    a) Conventional or traditional businesses.

    b) Mail order, telephone and internet marketing.

    c) Direct selling like Avon or Electrolux.

    d) MLM. Two kinds of business opportunities: Retail and wholesale.

3. Let us study the law of leverage

4. The three "S": The main foundation to success in MLM

5. Who are your prospects?

Yourself:

Others:

Never done MLM previously

Involved in MLM before

i) Those who may have had a bad experience.
ii) In the business before and are waiting for a new company to find them.
iii) Distributors from pyramid schemes.
iv) The so called leaders, who had a strong leader under them.
v) The ones who tell you they have ten years experience.

People from other companies

i) Still actively involved in the business.
ii) The uplines of the above.

6. Speed of sponsoring

Story: Tiger Woods Vs. Paul Azinger for the year 1999

For the average 18 holes, Woods plays 69.56 vs. 71.49 for Azinger
For putting, Woods averages 29.25 vs. 29.51 for Azinger
Tee-off distance, Woods averages 293 yards vs. 273 yards for Azinger
Income was US$6 million for Woods vs. US$500,000 for Azinger

7. The 5 lines 5 leaders system

a) Work on these 5 lines.
b) Find at least 5 leaders from these lines.
c) Find new lines to replace them and keep on growing.
d) Teach your leaders to duplicate this system.

8. Points to note

a) Use the ABC method.
b) Learn how to do the one-to-one OPP.
c) Start organizing home meetings and parties.
d) Be prepared.
e) Learn how to answer objections.
f) Have the good habits of sponsoring four people a week.

9. After an OPP, there will be two kinds of prospects

Those who want to join the business

a) Help them sign up.
b) Provide schedule of meetings to attend.
c) Provide audio, video tapes and literature.
d) Teach them how to start a prospect list.
e) Prepare them for discouragement.

Those who are still undecided

a) Find out why they are hesitant to join. Answer their objections.
b) Give him/her follow up material.
c) Encourage them by showing your commitment.
d) Provide them with exciting news when the opportunity arises.

10. Conclusion

a) Never give up because some of your prospects do not join.
b) Make a commitment to do the business for at least one year.

Story: The Principle of "Next"

Workshop on sponsoring:

Play 1. Get audience on stage to see the power of leverage.

Play 2: Two persons betting on a game of golf.

Quote:

Apple seed... Confucius

Quote:

1% vs. 100%...Paul Getty

Lesson 6
The ABC rule

1. Introduction

First of all, **ABC** stands for:

A = Advisor. All uplines, higher pin leaders, cross lines and the company.

B = Bridge. Yourself.

C = Customers. Your prospects.

2. Purpose of the ABC rule

a) Until you have mastered the skill of presenting the OPP and other training sessions, you should whenever possible and convenient to your advisors, act as the 'bridge' and let them do it for you. Please take note of the words, "convenient to your advisor." Do not be too demanding, thinking your advisor owes you and should always be on 24-hour standby. To all advisors out there, I do understand that you may be busy or over-worked, but this does not mean laziness or not pushing yourself hard enough.

Over the last twenty years, I have never allowed my new front lines ('B') to do the first five meetings themselves. The first few opportunity meetings have been done by me, as part of my commitment to them, since they are still new in the business. Normally, I do more than ten meetings – if you think that my business is big because I am lucky, please think again. I work very hard.

b) The ABC rule should also be used, when you have to communicate with people who are very close to you. For example, relatives, friends and colleagues, even if you think you already know what to do but you are still fairly new in the business. Use your 'A' if it is convenient, as they will listen more to your 'A' than you. Remember the Chinese saying, *"A monk from a foreign country knows how to teach the scriptures better."*

c) Also use the ABC system whenever you feel that the background of 'C' is better than your own, perhaps because of age, position, wealth or MLM experience.

d) Utilizing team power is more effective. For example, your 'A' does the marketing plan and you do the products and closing, so that your prospect is not listening to only one person for too long.

3. How to be a good 'A'

a) A good 'A' must understand the company, products and plan.
b) A good 'A' must be knowledgeable about MLM.
c) A good 'A' must know how to use and teach the ABC rule, so that 'B' can eventually take over leadership as another 'A'. The more 'A's there are in the group, the better.
d) A good 'A' must regularly attend training sessions, listen to tapes and read books.
e) A good 'A' must develop charisma.
f) A good 'A' must always be enthusiastic and excited.
g) A good 'A' must make it a habit to give 'B' confidence.
h) A good 'A' must show up, even when 'C' cancels the appointment.

4. How to be a good 'B'

a) A good 'B' must never interrupt when 'A' is communicating to 'C'. Keep quiet, pay attention and listen.
b) A good 'B' must take notes, record the conversation and have a
c) good learning attitude.
d) A good 'B' must not leave their seat and walk around when a
e) meeting is in progress.
f) A good 'B' must smile.
g) A good 'B' must turn off their cell phone or pager. Note the word "off", not silent or vibration mode. Off.

5. How to use the ABC rule

a) Before 'A' and 'C' meet, 'B' must give 'A' as much information as possible about 'C', using F.O.R.M. 'B' must spend a little time, say 5 - 10 minutes, in order to discuss with 'A', what 'C's needs may be.

b) 'B' selects the time and place for appointment and makes the invitation. Try to avoid using 'C's venue, unless it is their home. If possible, try to have 'C' seated facing the wall in a public place, so as to avoid any distractions.

c) 'B' reconfirms the appointment with 'C' the day before.

d) Tee-up. For those of you who play golf, you will understand the importance of a tee, a small little peg about 2 inches (5 centimeters) in length, made either of wood or plastic, where the golf ball is placed prior to teeing-off with the driver. Without this tee, even professional golfers can have problems trying to hit the golf ball with their drivers. It is therefore very important when 'A' and 'C' finally meet, that 'B' makes a big effort to tee-up 'A' during the introduction. Tee-up 'A' properly with excitement and praise and 'C' will inherently listen more attentively. 'B' must never tee-up 'C' and treat them like a VIP, because they are a prospect.

Here is a story for you to enjoy, so that you will never ever forget what tee-up is about.

Story: Tiger Woods

On a golf tour in Ireland, Tiger Woods drives his BMW into a petrol station in a remote part of the Irish countryside. The pump attendant, knowing nothing about golf, greets him in a typical Irish manner, completely unaware of the identity of the golfing pro. "Top of the mornin' to yer, sir," says the attendant. Tiger nods a quick "hello" and bends forward to pick up the nozzle. As he does so, two tees fall out of his shirt pocket onto the ground. "What are those?" asks the attendant. "They're called tees," replies Tiger. "Well, what on the good earth are they for?" inquires the Irishman. "They're for resting my balls on, when I'm driving," says Tiger. "Sweet Jaysus," says the Irishman, "BMW tinks of everythin'!"

Example:

Mr. 'B': "Tom, this is my upline, Mr. 'A'. He is an expert in our industry and has been in the business for the last 15 years. He is also the most successful distributor and has the biggest organization in our company. We are very fortunate that I am able to get his help from his very busy schedule, to help me show the business to you. Listen and learn from him."

A = **B** = **C** (equal importance = wrong)
A = B = **C** (tee up C = wrong)
A = B = C (tee up A = correct)

Below is a real instance of where I was introduced to a new prospect by an inexperienced distributor. You can see how the meeting got off on the wrong foot:

Mr. 'B': "Eddy, this is Mr. 'C'. He is a very rich and successful business man and if he is willing to join us, he can definitely help our company, as there are many things we can learn from him."

e) During the presentation, 'B' should make it a habit to take notes, in order to show the importance of the discussion.

f) After 'A' has finished, 'B' can take over the signing of the application form, do some product demonstration or answer objections. I normally leave 'B' with 'C' if they are friends, or know each other well, and where they may be more comfortable if I am not around.

g) 'B' and 'A' should also discuss how to follow up on 'C'.

Outline for Lesson 6
The ABC rule

1. Introduction

ABC stands for Advisor, Bridge and Customers

2. Purpose of the ABC rule

a) Before mastering skill, let the Upline do it for you.

b) When communicating with people who are very close to you.

c) When the background of 'C' is better than yours.

d) Utilizing team power is more effective.

3. How to be a good 'A'

a) A good 'A' must understand the company, products and plan.

b) A good 'A' must be knowledgeable about MLM.

c) A good 'A' must know how to use and teach the ABC rule.

d) A good 'A' must always improve knowledge.

e) A good 'A' must develop charisma.

f) A good 'A' must always be enthusiastic and excited.

g) A good 'A' must make it a habit to give 'B' confidence.

h) A good 'A' must show up even when 'C' cancels the appointment.

4. How to be a good 'B'

a) A good 'B' must never interrupt when 'A' is presenting.

b) A good 'B' must take notes, record the conversation and learn.

c) A good 'B' must not leave their seat and walk around.

d) A good 'B' must smile.

e) A good 'B' must turn off their cell phone or pager.

5. How to use the ABC rule

a) 'B' must give 'A' as much information as possible about 'C', using F.O.R.M.

b) 'B' to select time and place for appointment and make the invitation.

c) 'B' to reconfirm the appointment with 'C' the day before.

d) Tee-up 'A'.

e) During the presentation, 'B' should make it a habit to take notes.

f) After 'A' has finished, 'B' can try to take over.

g) 'B' and 'A' should also discuss how to follow up on 'C'.

Lesson 7
Follow up

1. Introduction

I would like to divide the follow up, into four types:

Follow up yourself.

Follow up new distributors who have just registered.

Follow up your upline.

Follow up customers.

2. Yourself

I would ask you to follow up on yourself, before you follow up on others, so that you can make the process of following up effective and fun. What I want is for you to develop the habit of checking yourself first, whether it be in sponsoring, follow up, or retailing, because I often see distributors not being very effective, due to lack of commitment and their belief systems not being 100%. I also see leaders who have not followed up on themselves properly, and who as a result say the wrong things, teach the wrong things, and do the wrong things. I sometimes joke with second-rate distributors, that sometimes I wish they did less, because the more they do, the smaller the organization becomes!

I am sure you can see how ineffective distributors will be, when they try to follow up with new distributors, without having even made up their own minds that they are really committed to the business. Can you imagine the things they will say to the prospect? The same poor result can be seen when they follow up with their upline and customers. For follow up on yourself, observe the following:

a) Why did you join the business?

b) Set your goals (daily, weekly and monthly).

c) Listen to one tape per week.

d) Attend as many meetings as you can.

e) Keep an up-to-date 20 name prospect list at all times.

f) Use all the company products.

g) Retail products to 10 to 20 customers a month.

h) Keep some stock.

i) Keep a financial account of your business.

j) Phone your uplines and downlines every day.

k) Start writing your training notes.

l) Print your business card.

3. For new prospects and distributors

Normally when we talk about follow up, most of us think about follow up for new distributors. It is very important that a distributor, after spending the time to talk to a prospect about the business, must also spend time to follow up, whether the prospect registers or not.

If the prospect does not register, it may be because they need more of your time to help them overcome some of their doubts. They may need you to answer some of their objections, and/or have more information. Maybe, they do not want to register the first time they see the business, even though they are very interested. Many of us do not place an order on a new car the first time we visit the showroom, even though we are longing to have it in our garage.

If they register, your work has just begun. Within 48 hours, all responsible uplines must spend time with the new downlines, to increase the new distributor's understanding of the business. There are many areas you have to cover. I would love to see all good sponsors, give new distributors a further and more in-depth explanation of their company's marketing plan. If you feel that you already gave an in-depth and detailed presentation the first time, I would suggest that you are not doing your first presentation right! For the follow up, you may want to talk about your company's incentives, and where applicable, their profit sharing program. You must also spend time on the products, unless of course your company is a pyramid scheme, in which event, emphasis on product is not important!

Talk about your company, the people, the President or even the industry, using some of the information I gave you in the first few lessons to this book.

When you show the business, what you do is to show your prospect the features that are offered by your company, and from the features they will decide if they are interested in the benefits. However, many times after registering, new distributors do nothing simply because of doubt, or because they do not know what to do. It is of the utmost importance that you help new distributors overcome their doubts, and that you start to give them instructions on doing things to get them moving. You may once in a while come across a 'fire starter', who only needs a little spark from a match to get going; and very soon the whole place is on fire! But the majority of the time, your new downline is not this type. They are coals. To be a good sponsor, you must give your new distributor commitment during your follow up, and build your new line like a professional, by teaching them a good system, and the spirit and culture of your group. You are the 'fire starter' and you must use your fire to burn the coals, and to slowly fan the coals until you have a big fire.

Rule:

Features = Benefits = Needs = Doubt = No action

What can sometimes happen, is that the sponsor may have shown the great features of an OPP., leaving the prospect excited about the benefits and how they satisfy their needs. But if the sponsor does not follow up properly, sometimes this 'fired-up' prospect goes home and the fire soon starts to smolder. Doubts creep in about whether this is a feasible business; doubt about whether they can be successful. Many things may rain on the inferno that was so hot. Some people have never succeeded in anything, and now they want to go into a business of their own? Sometimes it may be overwhelming, and they begin to have doubts, and doubt will lead to inaction.

Be excited when you follow up with your new downline, but you must have the knowledge, and if you don't, ask your upline for help. Again, use the ABC method. Your knowledgeable upline is now the 'A', you become the 'B' and your new distributor the 'C'.

Story: Duck eggs versus chicken eggs

When you compare a duck egg with a chicken egg, you will immediately notice that the duck egg is bigger. Tests have proven that a duck egg is more nutritious then a chicken egg. Break the two eggs, and you will also see that the yolk of the duck egg is firmer and better looking. If you cook the two eggs, you will find that duck eggs taste better.

But ask yourself which sells the best, chicken eggs or duck eggs? Answer, chicken eggs. Why?

Because when a duck lays an egg, there is no excitement. On the other hand, when a hen lays an egg, she will flap her feathers, fly around and holler, as if to tell everyone, "I've laid an egg! I've laid an egg! Come and buy!"

4. What to do during follow up

Follow up on a new distributor is not a one-time thing. You must do it over a period of time, and you must do the following:

a) Lead your downline. They should not lead you. Spend 80% of your time on that person, if you think they are a potential leader.

b) You must know how to teach your new line.

c) Check on their progress.

d) Help them to solve problems and give them encouragement.

e) Help them to set goals. Help your downline to dream.

f) Make sure they read and listen to appropriate books and tapes.

g) See to it that they attend meetings, trainings and rallies, and that they start sponsoring.

h) That they maintain a prospect list.

i) If they have challenges in getting prospects, check on their invitation skills.

j) Fix a weekly OPP. for your downline

k) Report only good news, never bad news

Rule: Report good and bad news to your upline, but only good news to your downline.

l) Always compliment your downlines and if you find that difficult, because you think there is nothing to compliment, then shut up!

5. Follow- up your 'A'

a) Be humble, have a good learning attitude and learn to solve problems, after learning from 'A'.

b) You must phone your 'A' at least once a week, and teach all your downlines to do the same, as part of your group culture - you will be glad you did. One of the most common mistakes made by many downlines, is that they think they know more then their 'A' and as a result, they do not even bother to contact their 'A'. Can you imagine what will happen when a group has this spirit and culture? When you have a big group as the 'A', if all your downlines phone you, everyone only needs to make one call. If all the downlines only wait for you to call, you will have no time for anything else!

c) Find time to see 'A', at 'A's convenience.

d) Ask questions if you face challenges, but do not whine and talk negatives. Learn to recognize and differentiate between the two.

e) Be excited and report good news, as your 'A' needs a lift too.

f) Check on your company and distributor center schedule and events.

6. Follow-up for customers

We will deal with this in the topic, 'How to retail.'

7. Psychology of follow-up:

Help other people get what they want and you will get what you want.

Outline for Lesson 7
Follow up

1. Introduction

Four types:

Follow up yourself.

Follow up new distributors who have just registered.

Follow up your upline.

Follow up customers.

2. Yourself

a) Why did you join the business?

b) Set your goals (Daily, weekly and monthly).

c) Listen to one tape per week.

d) Attend as many meetings as you can.

e) Keep a 20+ name prospects list.

f) Use all the company products.

g) Retail to 10 to 20 customers a month.

h) Keep some stock.

i) Keep a financial account of your business.

j) Phone your uplines and downlines every day.

k) Start writing your training notes.

l) Print your business card.

3. For new distributors

Follow up whether the prospect registers or not.

If the prospect does not register, help them overcome their doubts.

If they register, start to teach within 48 hours.

Be a good sponsor; be the fire starter.

Story: Duck eggs versus chicken eggs

Rule: Features = Benefits = Needs = Doubt = No action

4. What to do during follow up

a) Lead downline. They should not lead you. 80% of time on leader.

b) You must know how to teach your new line.

c) Check on their progress.

d) Help them solve problems and give encouragement.

e) Help them set goals. Help your downline dream.

f) Make sure they read and listen to appropriate books and tapes.

g) Check they attend events and starts sponsoring.

h) They maintain a prospect list.

i) Check on their invitation skills.

j) Fix a weekly OPP for your downline.

k) Report only good news, never bad news.

l) Always compliment your downlines.

5. Follow- up your 'A'

a) Be humble. Good learning attitude. Solve problems after learning.

b) Phone your 'A' at least once a week.

c) Find time to see 'A', at 'A's convenience.

d) Ask questions. Do not whine and talk negatives.

e) Be excited and report good news.

f) Check on company and distributor center schedule and events.

6. Follow-up for customers

We will deal with this in the topic, 'How to retail'

7. Psychology of follow-up

Help other people get what they want and you will get what you want.

Lesson 8
M.A.M. (Meeting after Meeting)

1. Introduction

A 'Meeting after Meeting' or M.A.M., is divided into two types:

> M.A.M. after Opp.
> M.A.M. after a training or rally.

The purpose of a MAM is similar to that of follow up, except that it is done immediately after an event; that is, after an OPP, training or rally.

2. M.A.M. after a business opportunity meeting

There are four points I try and sell for an MAM after a business opportunity meeting, namely:

a) Ways of doing business

Tell new prospects the different ways of doing business. You may be surprised that after all the time the speaker has spent at the OPP, showing the beauty of our business and how we can leverage our time through others, some prospects will still think it is a door-to-door business and not register. However, for those who love to sell and want to register, because they think it is a door-to-door business, great, but I sure hate to lose a prospect, simply because they are turned off by the idea of selling. So to start my MAM, I talk on the three different kinds of businesses:

  i) Conventional businesses. The many challenges they must face. Investment, experience required and risk.

  ii) Direct selling, where salespeople are not allowed to leverage their time.

  iii) MLM is actually two kinds of business opportunity; a retail and a wholesale opportunity.

Here, I also contrast the difference between direct selling and MLM, where we are given the opportunity to use the power of leverage to help us build a bigger and more stable business:

1 salesman x 100 customers = 100 customers (single level direct selling)
What if the salesman fractures a leg and cannot work for a month?

1 distributor x 10 distributors = 10 distributors x 10 distributors = over 100 distributors x 20 customers = over 2,000 customers (MLM)
If the leader fractures a leg, the business still goes on.

I also touch on the 3 'S', which you will remember is the most important secret to success in MLM. Again, on this point, I touch on the importance of the wholesale business and that retailing is very important; the difference in our business being that it is about a lot of people each servicing 10 to 20 customers. The lifeblood of MLM is people, and people come as a result of sponsoring. However, I do not want you to think that I am teaching you that retailing is not important. It is very important, but I prefer you to sponsor your prospects first, and retail to them second (if they are not interested in the business opportunity), rather than vice versa.

S = sponsor   = 50%
S = sale   = 50%
S = service   = 100%

b) The ABC Rule

The next thing I do is to explain the ABC rule. The purpose of this is to give comfort to new distributors, to make them aware that we know they need help to get started, but that they need not fear, as we will do at least the first 5 meetings for them. The opposite of fear is courage, and courage is doing what you fear.   Keep ABC very basic.

c) Invitation

Teach your new prospect the basic art of invitation. Keep it very simple. Do not at this stage go through the whole Lesson on invitation.

d) Discouragement

Prepare them for discouragement from:

People who care about you.

People who are failures themselves.

Distributors from other MLM companies.

You must keep your MAM under 15 to 20 minutes, as your prospect has already sat through a presentation, which may have lasted an hour to an hour-and-a-half. Keep the four points simple and basic.

3. Action:

After going through the four points, you must take the following actions:

a) Help those who are interested to register and/or order products. Thank those who are not interested, and see if they are willing to become customers. Do not force the business on your prospects, but let them make their own intelligent decision. You have already done your job, by showing them the business. Make sure your prospects are happy and comfortable, even if they do not want to be involved, because you should already be grateful and honored that they have given you their time. Be sincere about it. Ask them for leads.

b) Answer objections. Do not let the prospect take their doubts home. Communicate ideas.

c) Arrange next appointment (within 48 hours).

d) It is normal for some new distributors who have just registered, to be very excited and want to ask questions and not go home. Teach them how get started in the business, and find time to give them an opportunity to talk or introduce themselves, and you will be glad you did. Ask them what attracts them in the business, and let them set simple goals. Most importantly, let them talk. It is always a joy to listen to this group of people. They always make my day and I go home smiling.

4. Points to note:

a) Do not put down other people's decision or occupations.

b) Do not criticize other MLM companies. It is amazing to sometimes observe the amount of time distributors from different companies spend, criticizing each other. Do not forget that when we do this, we are really telling people about what is bad in our industry, and when we are finished, we wonder why the new prospect does not want to register.

c) Do not over-emphasize that we are not a pyramid scheme. The more you do, the worse the effect, and the more you try and convince people that we are not a pyramid scheme, the more we sound like one.

d) Our new prospects come from different backgrounds. Try to see how our business can fulfill their needs, not yours. The six basic needs are:

>   certainty / comfort
>   uncertainty / variety
>   significance
>   connection and love
>   growth
>   contribution

You can read more on this subject in Anthony Robbins's books.

e) Pay attention to details, and prepare what you are going to say in advance. Here are some examples you can use to help you open the conversation:

"This business is really great. Now you know why I am so excited."

"What part interests you the most about our marketing plan?"

"I would really like to help you sponsor this week; who do you think would be your best prospect?"

"I am sure this business will help make your dreams come true."

"After what you have just heard, is there any further information I can give you?"

Confident = Enthusiastic = Smile

f) Give some follow-up material, such as audio, video tape, CD, sales literature, etc., to your new downline and make another appointment for within 48 hours. Follow-up material will provide more information about your company, and give you a reason to follow-up your prospect.

5. MAM after rallies or training (sizzling sessions)

I have been extremely blessed that today my group is very big, and as a result I organize regular rallies and trainings. This allows my leaders and I to hold 'sizzling sessions' after these events. If your group does not get together regularly, because you or your company do not have regular rallies and trainings, you must still organize this once-a-month sizzling session for your group.

However, I have divided the MAM after a rally into two types, as many distributors also bring their prospects to rallies, even though they have never seen the Opp. Some may even bring new prospects to training meetings, but that is not normal or advisable.

a) New Prospects (Opp)

It is normal for many distributors to invite their friends and relatives to attend rallies, even before they have seen the business. What must you do, immediately after the rally?

    i) Introduce distributors to the VIP speakers and other high pin distributors, and take photos.

    ii) Find a location to give a one-to-one OPP to the new people.

b) For Distributors and also new prospects (Sizzling session)

If you decide to do an OPP to the new prospect at a later date, you can also put them in a MAM that we call a sizzling session.

Normally, my leaders arrange meeting venues where we hold the rally, or at facilities nearby, for this very important sizzling session after the rally. As most of my groups are rather big, these venues normally sit about 100 to 500 people, and over 1,000 for certain huge groups. To save money, leaders should try and use their own center, if it is not too far from the rally venue or inconvenient for the distributors. For up-and-coming leaders, whose groups are still small, I will still insist that they hold this very important MAM, even if it is just for a handful of distributors. You can do it anywhere; a coffee shop, hotel lobby, your home, their home, or even in the parking lot of the rally venue.

6. What to do for this MAM or sizzling session?

a) Have new people introduce themselves, or let their sponsor introduce them. Some may be shy but you will be surprised at the number of new prospects who are excited about the rally and make a commitment to do the business. If there are too many new people to introduce, you must at least give them a warm welcome. People love recognition.

b) Have distributors share their testimony of what they heard in the rally. This can be a wonderful way to start training new distributors on how to speak in public. Keep a sharp eye on new potential leaders, and normally you can see them shine during these sessions.

c) Whenever possible, I like to make it a habit to invite a cross-line leader to share or help. I will select a topic for the invited guest to speak on.

d) I also use this sizzling session, to sell the spirit and culture of the group, in order to help foster a team identity.

e) I like to conclude by letting the leaders do some goal setting, and instruction on what I would like to achieve for the week or month.

Note: All distributors must learn how to do meeting-after-meetings and be able to work independently when no help is available.

You must organize this sizzling session once a month for your group. Sizzling sessions can also be done after rallies or training sessions, or at any time convenient to the group.

7. Conclusion

Story: The tightrope walker

A tightrope walker one day announced that he intended to perform a special feat, pulling a steel cable across Niagara Falls, and then walking across the falls from the Canadian to the American side.

No one believed he could do such a feat, especially a reporter who wrote in the newspaper that the tightrope walker was crazy.

The acrobat announced that he was going to perform his feat one Sunday. Many people came to watch and he successfully walked across the Falls. When he was on stage being congratulated, he saw the reporter and immediately asked him if he now believed, or did he still believe he was crazy. The reporter replied that he now believed, as he had seen the feat accomplished.

The tightrope walker then told the reporter that not only could he do this feat but he was also confident that he could tie a special chair on his back, invite his assistant to sit on the chair, and then still do the same feat. He asked the reporter whether he believed it could be done. To this, the reporter replied that he did not believe it could be done, and that he was crazy.

The tightrope walker announced to the audience that he would attempt this feat the following Sunday.

With all the newspaper and TV coverage, thousands came the following Sunday to see him and his assistant perform this difficult feat, and again the tightrope walker was successful.

When he was on stage, again he saw the reporter and asked him whether he now believed. The reporter congratulated him and said that he now believed, as he had seen the feat with his own two eyes.

The tightrope walker then asked the reporter again, "Do you really believe?" The reporter said, "Yes", as he had seen the feat accomplished.

The tightrope walker then said to him, "Reporter, if you really believe, climb up on my chair."

Close:
"I hope you have enjoyed your visit today and like what you have seen. If you believe what you have seen, I would like to invite you to climb up on my chair. Let us work together, and let me help you turn your dreams into reality."

Outline for Lesson 8
M.A.M. (Meeting after Meeting)

1. Introduction

Meeting after Meeting or M.A.M. is divided into two types.
    M.A.M. after Opp.
    M.A.M. after a training or rally.

2. M.A.M. after a business opportunity meeting

Four points I sell:
a) Ways of doing business:
    i) Conventional businesses.
    ii) Direct selling.
    iii) MLM. Retail and Wholesale.

b) The ABC Rule
c) Invitation
d) Discouragement:
    People who care about you.
    People who are failures themselves.
    Distributors from other MLM companies.

Keep your MAM under 15 to 20 minutes.

3. Action

a) Help interested prospects to register and/or order products. Thank those not interested.
b) Answer objections.
c) Arrange next appointment (within 48 hours).
d) Teach the excited how to get started in the business. Let them talk.

4. Points to note

a) Do not put down other people's decision or occupations.
b) Do not criticize other MLM companies.
c) Do not over-emphasize that we are not a pyramid scheme.
d) Our new prospects six basic needs are:
   certainty / comfort
   uncertainty / variety
   significance
   connection and love
   growth
   contribution
e) Pay attention to details. Be prepared.
   Confident = Enthusiastic = Smile
f) Give follow-up material. Make another appointment within 48 hours.

5. MAM after rallies or training (sizzling sessions)

Two types:
a) New Prospects (Opp)
   i) Introduce distributors to the VIP speakers and other high pin distributors.
   ii) Find a location and give a one-to-one OPP to the new people

b) For Distributors and also new prospects (sizzling session).
Organize this sizzling session once a month for your group.

6. What to do for this MAM or sizzling session?

a) Introduce new people.
b) Have distributors share their testimony.
c) Invite a guest speaker if possible.
d) Sell the spirit and culture of the group, to help foster a team identity.
e) Let the leaders do some goal setting. Give instructions.

7. Conclusion

Story: The tightrope walker

Lesson 9
How to Retail

1. Introduction

Retailing is the foundation stone of any form of marketing and without it, all companies are doomed to failure. Retailing therefore is not an option. If you are a distributor and you do not like to retail, we have good news for you - just do it anyway!

a) Traditional or conventional businesses have to sell

In conventional business, we talk about how manufactured goods go to wholesalers, who then sell these goods to area agents, who in turn sell to middlemen, and from them to retail stores, who in turn then sell to customers.

Imagine a scenario where the manufacturer, wholesalers, area agents, middlemen, and retail store owners all did not sell, but only bought the goods for personal use. Imagine the same thing happening in your organization, where all of your downlines and you yourself, do not like retailing and buy products only for personal use. How successful will your business be? Sure, I know that when you sponsor others into the organization, it is also part of retailing but let me assure you, that if you want to be big and stable, you have to teach all your downlines to sell to 10 to 20 customers every month. It is really simple mathematics and common sense. If you have 1,000 distributors and they all buy for personal use, and another leader also has 1,000 distributors who in turn sell to 10 to 20 customers every month, who has a bigger and healthier business? With all the active sponsored distributors looking after a large customer base, your organization will be solid.

b) Pyramid schemes do not have customers

One of the ways to identify a pyramid scheme, is that they only have distributors but no customers, and the reason is simple. When you have a scheme that plays the money game, the products are grossly overpriced, and any person in their right mind will have no reason to buy the products. Only distributors buy products, not because they want or need them, but because they are required to do so in order to maintain the distributorship. It is therefore normal for these types of companies to tell prospects that they only need to sign up, pay however many dollars, and that no retailing is required. I hope your company is not one of those but if it is, get out fast!

c) Retailing keeps the organization healthy
Retailing to customers will not only bring your organization the retail profit, but also the other bonuses built into the marketing plan, and this will keep your organization healthy with money. You need this new money from customers to keep your organization healthy. If you do not teach retailing to your organization, and only emphasize sponsoring and personal use, the distributors in your organization will become poorer and poorer after a period of time.

As a restaurant owner, I made it a habit to visit a few restaurants close by my place on a regular basis, both to enjoy myself and to do some public relations with the restaurant owners. After all, my place happened to be the most successful, and it's important to maintain peace with the neighbors. These owners all became very good friends, and they also came to my place on a regular basis. Do you think we could have survived and paid the business overheads, if we only ate in each other's place, and only made money from each other, without making money from customers?

Your distributors also have many expenses to pay for every month - the mortgage, rent, car payment, credit cards, bills, the children, etc. All these take money out of the pool, and you need new money from the customers to come into this pool every month. The same applies to all other businesses and professions.

Workshop: Poker friends

Let us imagine four friends who have a habit of playing poker every night and who each start with US$1,000. Every night, everyone takes out US$30 from their US$1,000 to buy supper and drinks. After 30 days, there is no winner or loser. Guess how much money each player has got left in their pocket after 30 days? Take 10 seconds to calculate and another 10 minutes to think how you and your group are doing the business today!

2. How to retail?

Because retailing is such an important part of the business, you must learn to remember every one of the points that follow:

a) First retail to yourself

Before you start to retail to others, please remember what I always want you to do first. You must first of all retail to yourself. Use your company products to see how good they are and how much you like and believe in them on quality and price. Check to see if the products carry a guarantee. You have to remember that in order to be a good multi-level marketer, it is more than just about making money. You have to be accountable to your customers, and many of these people are friends of yours and people you know. If you do not believe in the products, you may want to find a new company.

All good MLM companies must take the responsibility to source good products for their distributors and to have them fairly priced. MLM companies, in truth, only have one customer, the distributor. They cannot sell to anybody else. A person can be the richest person in town, but unless they join your company and become a distributor, they can only buy from you or other distributors. Isn't this great? Owners of MLM companies need to be fair, not too greedy, and to treat their distributors well, as they are their only customers.

b) Be a professional

Be a professional and take the business seriously. I have a distributor who once sold a tube of toothpaste to a customer, and who later received a call from the customer to ask why the toothpaste was green in color and not white. It was green because it was supposed to be green, but because the distributor did not use the product herself, she told the customer to return it, as she also thought the toothpaste should be white! I think you will agree that she was not very professional. Below is a story you may enjoy:

Story: Landmines

An American teacher spent many years teaching in Vietnam and while he was there, one of the things that bothered him was that the men walked in front, while the women walked behind. He always told his Vietnamese friends that in America, the women walked in front, and that they too should adopt the 'Ladies first policy.'

Nobody listened to him, and he returned to the USA when the Vietnam War broke out.

After the war, he returned to Vietnam and to his surprise, all the women now walked in front, and the men behind. He was so happy, thinking that finally he had succeeded in teaching all the Vietnamese men to adopt this Western culture.

He kept boasting about his success, until finally a Vietnamese friend told him, "Teacher, we let our women walk in front now, because the Viet Cong planted so many landmines throughout the country."

If you are not using the products yet, why not? Are you afraid of landmines? Are your company products that bad?

c) Be prepared

Again, be a professional and be prepared before you meet your customers. Make sure that you have the following:

i) You must have your product demonstration kit and brochures on hand for demonstration. By the way, do not forget to learn how to do a product demonstration, before you demonstrate for a customer.

Once, a young lady did a demo with shoe polish. She was supposed to only apply a bit of shoe polish to the palm of her hand, and to then apply a tiny dollop of liquid soap to clean it. Instead, she put a whole handful of shoe polish into her palm! There was no way a tiny application of soap was going to clean off that much shoe polish. She ended up with black polish covering both her hands! So practice your demo before you perform for others.

ii) Keep some stock on hand, as some customers may have the urge to buy when they see that the products are immediately available.

d) Sell to 10 to 20 customers every month

You must set your goal to sell to 10 to 20 customers every month, and teach your downlines to do the same. Keep a detailed customer file, and estimate when they might be running out of products. A computer will be a great help here.

Check yourself and your group. All leaders who only order products at the end of the month to maintain their minimum requirement, are also leaders who do not emphasize the importance of selling in their organization, because they are themselves poor in retailing. They have no stock at home, and have no loyal customers who they regularly service. Their business is on the borderline, and their commitment is not strong.

e) Work from home (Product Parties)

Work from the convenience of your home or the home of downlines, friends and relatives. Organize Product Parties (PP) and offer gifts or prizes as incentives. More will be written on PP in Book 2, as PP normally takes place because a higher pin leader is helping to organize it.

f) Ask for the sale

Ask for sales, as you are sharing good products with friends and relatives. The Bible says, "Ask and it shall be given, seek and you will find."

   i) Ask your customers to change brands. Ask them for help, because you are starting a new business, and you will be surprised how many of your friends and relatives love and care for you. It reads both ways.

   ii) Tell them about your company money-back guarantee.

   iii) Offer to deliver products to their home, especially to the elderly, who may need this service. Emphasize safety in purchasing from you as a known person, rather than products delivered by strangers. At the time of writing this book, there is a terrible outbreak of the SARS virus (Severe Acute Respiratory Syndrome) and people are avoiding department stores and public places. Our direct delivery system of many products, is definitely an added plus to many worried people, especially when most MLM companies sell 'wellness' products.

g) Sell products based on customer's needs

Sell products based on customer's needs and when selling, respect your customer's time.

h) Personal sticker

Put your personal sticker on the products you sell, to better your customer service.

i) Accounts

Separate your personal cash from your product account.

3. Do not:

a) Do not exaggerate product quality or any money back guarantee.
b) Do not make medical claims.
c) Do not argue with customers. The customer is 'King'.
d) Do not criticize the products of other companies.
e) Do not undercut established prices. At this point, I must spend some time on this issue of discounting, even though I know it is a problem that is very difficult to solve:

4. Discounting

From time to time over the last 20 years, I have received calls from anxious distributors whose customers have found another distributor offering the products at a discounted price. Sometimes, the discount price being offered is little more than wholesale, and I have even come across discounting that is below the distributor price; in other words, the distributor is even giving back the bonuses. Discounting is not against most company policies, because it is unlawful for manufacturers or distributors to fix retail prices in countries having a consumer protection price fixing law. Therefore companies can only have a suggested retail price (SRP).

However, all distributors must know that discounting damages the reputation of the company as a whole, and fellow distributor in particular. It will confuse the customers and devalues the product. It will also create disharmony amongst distributors. Perhaps the most damaging effect of all is that distributors no longer dare sell at SRP, for fear that if their customers find out that the products can be bought cheaper, they may feel they are being cheated.

So why are distributors doing it? I can think of a few reasons:
a) The distributor does not believe in the value of the products.

b) The distributor does not have business sense, and feels uncomfortable making money from people they know. Maybe it is because it is MLM, since they would presumably have no problem making a retail profit from their friends and relatives, if they owned a grocery store or a travel agency and had 'real' expenses.

c) Playing games, results in excessive inventory of products, where for example, the focus of the business is simply going for the pin, or pushing the envelope to unethically qualify for certain special incentives, and not the business itself.

d) The distributor does not emphasize on retailing and as a result, does not have a customer base to absorb the minimum requirement, which is required by the company in order to be entitled to bonuses.

e) The distributor has not reached the level of maturity, and as a result, does not understand the love and care for the greater good of the company.

5. Solution:

a) The easiest, of course, is to stop this destructive attitude and to sell at SRP. The group leaders must make great efforts to teach and check their group. They are probably the only people who can stop this unhealthy practice. By the way, they are also the main people who cause it. One of the rules in MLM, is that when leaders do not stop an unhealthy situation, they are encouraging it. Never forget this rule. I will come down harder on leaders in Books 2 and 3 on this rule. You have not heard the last of it yet!

b) The other alternative, which I still do not like, but will suggest anyway, is to give the discount not in the SRP, but in giving more products. For example, if a customer bought 10 bottles of shampoo at US$10 each; 10 bottles x US$10 = US$100. Instead of giving them a 20% or US$20 discount, I would rather you give them another 2 bottles of shampoo.

6. Follow up

a) Thank your customer for the order. I would love to see all distributors who make a sale, write a small thank-you note to their customers.

Workshop:

Let us take 10 minutes, to write a great thank-you note to a customer who has bought something from you.

a) After you think they have received your letter, phone them up to see if they like the products, or need any help. You will be surprised by the number of customers who buy products from distributors, but do not know how to use those products.

b) Periodically phone your customers, to enquire about re-orders.

Rule: The first sale is not a sale; the second sale is a sale.

a) Invite them to product demos, sales promotion or introduction of new products, sponsored by the company or your upline. Send them new brochures, or inform them when new products are being introduced.

7. Psychology of retailing
Retailing in MLM is sharing, not pushing sales.

Sharing is easy when you make retailing a pleasure, not pain.

8. Conclusion

MLM may be a vehicle to your dreams, but it is not going to happen if you and your organization do not retail. So I would like to conclude this chapter, with this story:

Story: The life of the bird is in your hands

A boy caught a bird one day and decided to test the wisdom of the wise old man in the village. He went and saw the wise old man. Keeping the bird in his hand, behind his back, he asked, "Wise old man, I have a bird in my hand. Is it dead or alive?" Of course, the wise old man knew that if he told the boy that the bird was alive, he would squeeze it to death, and if he said the bird was dead, he would let it go. So the wise old man replied, "The life of the bird is in your hands."

The life of your business is also in your hands. You can choose to emphasize or not emphasize on retailing in your organization. Make a decision and do not discount.

Outline for Lesson 9
How to Retail

1. Introduction

Retailing is the foundation stone

Retailing therefore is not an option

a) Traditional or conventional businesses have to sell.
b) Pyramid schemes do not have customers.
c) Retailing keeps the organization healthy.

Workshop: Poker friends

2. How to retail

a) First retail to yourself.
b) Be a professional.

Story: Landmines

c) Be prepared. Make sure you have the following:
   i) Your product demonstration kit and brochures.
   ii) Keep some stock.
d) Sell to 10 to 20 customers every month.
e) Work from home. Organize Product Parties (PP).
f) Ask for the sale.
   i) Ask your customers to change brands.
   ii) Tell them about your company money-back guarantee.
   iii) Offer to deliver products to their home.
g) Sell products based on customer's needs, and when selling respect your customer's time.
h) Put your personal sticker on the products.
i) Separate your personal cash from your product account.

3. Do not

   a) Do not exaggerate product quality, or any money back guarantee.
   b) Do not make medical claims.
   c) Do not argue with customers. The customer is 'King'.
   d) Do not criticize the products of other companies.
   e) Do not undercut established prices.

4. Discounting

Discounting damages the reputation of the company and distributors.
Discounting confuses the customers and devalues the product.
Discounting creates disharmony amongst distributors.
Distributors no longer dare to sell at SRP.

So why are distributors doing it? I can think of a few reasons:
   a) The distributor does not believe in the value of the products.
   b) The distributor does not have the business sense.
   c) Playing games, resulting in overstock of products.
   d) The distributor has no customer base to absorb the monthly
      minimum requirement.
   e) The distributor has not reached the level of maturity.

5. Solution

   a) Leaders must stop it. By saying nothing, leaders are encouraging
      it.
   b) Give discount not in the SRP, but in giving more products.

6. Follow up

   a) Thank your customer for the order.

Workshop: Take 10 minutes to write a great

'thank- you' note to a customer

b) Phone them up to see if the like the products, or need any help.

c) Phone your customers about re-orders.

Rule: The first sale is not a sale; the second sale is a sale

d) Invite them to product demos, sales promotion or introduction of new products.

7. Psychology of retailing

Retailing in MLM is sharing, not pushing sales

8. Conclusion

Story: The life of the bird is in your hands

Lesson 10
Answering objections

1. Introduction

a) Expect questions and even objections.

MLM is a people business, and when we introduce new products or a new business opportunity to people, many of them may have no idea as to what is being offered, or have prior misconceptions as to what MLM is all about. You should expect them to ask questions, and even have objections. Your customers or prospects are not trying to be difficult - it is normal behavior and as salespeople, whether selling products, the business or ourselves, we should try to be professional problem-solvers. We can sometimes forget that an apparently silly question from a customer or prospect, seems that way only because we are more experienced than them. We will probably ask some silly questions ourselves, when other people want to sell us something we do not know about.

b) Be prepared and practice.

The best advice I can give you for this, is to be prepared. You will definitely excel in this area, once you know what questions may be asked and already know how to answer them, due to your experience, learning and practice. I have good news for you. There are only about 10 to 15 questions or objections that constantly come up, and all you have to do is to memorize the answers, and with practice, you will be an expert on this topic in no time at all.

2. Attitude and skill

a) Listen and digest questions. All leaders must do their best to listen and digest all questions, before attempting to give answers. Perhaps this is the reason why we are given two ears but only one mouth! One of the most common mistakes in communication is in not knowing what the other person is asking or thinking, and as a result, we end up giving the wrong answer, or coming to the wrong conclusion. Here is a story I hope you will enjoy:

Story: Moishe

A long time ago, the Pope decided that all Jews had to leave Rome. Naturally there was a big uproar from the Jewish community. So, the Pope made a deal. He would have a religious debate with a member of the Jewish community. If the Jew won, the Jews could stay, but if the Pope won, the Jews would leave.

The Jews, realizing that they had no choice, looked around for a champion to defend their faith, but no one wanted to volunteer. It was too risky. So they finally picked an old man named Moishe, who spent his life sweeping up after people. Being old and poor, he had nothing to lose, so he agreed. Because he was not used to talking very much, he asked for the debate to be subject to the condition that neither side be allowed to talk. The Pope agreed.

The day of the great debate arrived. Moishe and the Pope sat opposite each other for a full minute, before the Pope raised his hand and showed three fingers. Moishe looked back at him and raised one finger. The Pope waved his fingers in a circle around his head. Moishe pointed to the ground where he sat. The Pope pulled out a wafer and a glass of wine. Moishe pulled out an apple.

The Pope stood up and said, "I give up. This man is too good. The Jews can stay."

An hour later, the Cardinals gathered around the Pope, asking him what happened. The Pope said: "First I held up three fingers, to represent the Holy Trinity. He responded by holding up one finger, to remind me that there is still one God, common to both our religions."

"Then I waved my finger around me, to show him that God was all around us. He responded by pointing to the ground, showing that God is also right here with us."

"I pulled out the wine and the wafer, to show that God absolves us from our sins, but he pulled out an apple, to remind me of original sin."

"He had an answer for everything. What could I do?" sighed the Pope.

Meanwhile, the Jewish community had crowded around Moishe, amazed that this old, almost feeble-minded man, had done what all their scholars had insisted was impossible! "What happened?" they asked. "Well," said Moishe, "First, he said to me that the Jews had three days to get out of here, so I told him that not one of us was leaving.

Then he told me that this whole city would be cleared of Jews, but I let him know that we were staying right here."

"And then?" asked a woman. "I don't know," said Moishe. "He took out his lunch and I took out mine."

b) Do not exaggerate, and be sincere.

c) It is a two-way communication. Do not argue with your prospect or customer. I have never known a distributor who won a sale for arguing with a prospect or customer.

d) Always first accept their objections, and then give your proper answers.

e) Have the habit of using a 'tie-down' at the end of your answer. A tie-down is a question that demands a "Yes" answer. For example, "It is important to choose a good MLM company, isn't it?"

Here are some suggested tie-downs:

Isn't it?	Wasn't it?	Don't we?
Aren't they?	Isn't it true?	Won't they?
Haven't they?	Won't you?	Don't you agree?

3. Teach down

a)   You can increase your sales, by sponsoring more new distributors, but you can also increase your sales, by improving the selling skills of the distributors you already have. I believe the latter is very important, because it will lead to an increase in income for the people you already have in your organization. Don't you agree?

b)   You can increase your sales by devoting more hours to selling and getting more customers or you can increase your sales by improving both your own and your organization's selling skills.

c)   You can get distributors to stay in your organization by improving your communication skills, as you lead, talk and teach them as their leader. Answering objections is not limited to customers and new prospects, but extends to those same prospects, after they have joined the business as downlines.

4. Questions and objections to expect

a) Is it a pyramid scheme?
   I have good news for you. The majority of those who ask you this question do not know what a pyramid scheme is! They have a misconception, that when people do direct selling of goods or services through an organization where distributors can sponsor others to get benefits, it is a pyramid scheme, especially when the organization structure looks like a pyramid. The fact is, nearly all organizations only work effectively as a pyramid and are shaped like a pyramid. For example, in any big corporation, you may have a Chairman and CEO, and under that person, the President, followed by Vice Presidents, Managing Directors, General Managers, Assistant

General Managers, Managers, Assistant Managers, Supervisors, Assistant Supervisors, and the rest of the staff. Even Governments are structured this way. In the United States, there is the President, followed by the Vice President, and then the Secretaries of the various Departments which form the Cabinet.

When we come to think of it, even traditional businesses also take the form of a pyramid, where there is the Wholesaler or National Distributor (one), who sells to the Area Agents (a few), who in turn sell to the Middlemen (a dozen or so), on to Retail Stores (many), selling to the Customers. If a pyramid scheme is what most people misconceive it to be, then we are all involved in pyramid schemes.

Insurance companies also work the way we do, where an insurance salesperson can also sponsor and get benefits from other sales agents, so how come they are never accused of being involved in pyramid schemes?

In order for you to be able to explain a pyramid scheme, you must first of all know what a pyramid scheme is. One of the first identifying features of such schemes, is that they are designed to cheat people of their money, hence the public's fear and loathing. How then do they cheat and how do we identify them?

i)   The first thing all pyramid schemes do, is to insist that in order to become a member, there is a big registration fee and inventory loading. These schemes reward the sponsor an immediate 'finder's fee' for getting a new victim. Most registration fees will be of the order of US$500 to US$3,000, but I have even come across one, where the fee was US$30,000.

ii) Because a pyramid scheme is just a money game, the products are not important. Of course, nowadays it is very easy to find good products, so do not be surprised that many pyramid schemes also have excellent products. However, one thing I can guarantee you, is that these products will be overpriced, as the emphasis is not in retailing of products to customers, but rather in finding investors to play the money game.

iii) The easiest way to identify a pyramid scheme, is where they have distributors but no customers, and the only customers they have, are distributors who buy those products, because of their need to buy a distributorship to be involved in the scheme.

Other things to take note of, to help you identify pyramid schemes:

i) The next thing I am going to write will make some companies angry with me, but it comes from my observations over the years. Since there is no repeat purchase, because there are no customers, these kinds of pyramid companies tend to use the binary or triple matrix system, where in order to get certain benefits, the distributor buys more than one distributorship. Please note I am not saying all matrix based compensation companies are pyramid schemes; but it is a favored compensation model for pyramid schemes.

ii) They always emphasize making quick money in the shortest time possible.

iii) Beware of companies that claim you need not do anything after you have registered, you are paid a 'finder's fee', or that you only need to find another two or three victims.

iv) Stay away from companies that do not have a money back guarantee, or product return policy.

b) Market saturation

This is one of the easiest questions to answer, as you can tackle it from several angles:

i) "Since we sell consumable products, there will always be repeat sales, to ensure we do not have market saturation. Makes sense, doesn't it?"

ii) "Our company develops new products every year."

iii) "Every year in our country, there are xxx who reach an age to enter the job market (check the statistic in your country), so saturation is not possible."

iv) The figures below chart population growth from 1750 to the year 2000. It is interesting to note that in 1810, the world's population was only 1 billion. By 1930, it had grown to 2 billion, by 1960 to 3 billion and in the year 2000, it stood at over 6 billion!

1810 to 1930 = 120 years = 1 billion to 2 billion = 1 billion increase
1930 to 1960 =   30 years = 2 billion to 3 billion = 1 billion increase
1960 to 2000 =   40 years = 3 billion to 6 billion = 3 billion increase

We can see that the population is growing at a faster rate than ever before, and it is estimated that by the year 2020, the world's population will be 8 billion people. China alone is growing at the rate of 60,000 each day, for a net gain of about 16 million people per year, so I don't think saturation is a problem for us, do you?

v) "If you are worried about saturation, I have got good news for you. MLM is a business with no boundaries, our company is now opened in over xxx countries, and our international sponsoring program is such that you can now do business in all these countries. We will be expanding every year into new markets, so eventually the whole world of six billion people is your market. Watch out when we open up in China and India. These two big markets should interest you, don't you agree?"

c) Do I have to sell?

Before you answer this question, you must understand that some people like to sell, and some do not. One of the mistakes some leaders make, is in assuming that people who ask this question, do not like to sell, when it can happen that a prospect loves the idea of selling, because they are so impressed with the products. For this question, always ask, "do you like selling?" Then, if their answer is,

"Yes", your response can be, "Great, you will like this business, because we have over xxx products that you can sell." Or, if the answer is, "No", then you can say, "Great, you would like this business, because in MLM, we offer you a wholesale opportunity."

However, I want to remind all distributors that after joining the business, you have to look after 10 to 20 customers every month, and you must all learn to like selling, if you want your organization to be solid and profitable.

d) This business enriches the people who join at the ground floor
People sometimes question, whether MLM is a business that benefits only people who join first, perhaps feeling that they may now be too late, or that they would be better served to join a new company.
Answers:
   i)   If 'A' sponsors 'B' and has only one line but 'B', because he/she worked very hard, has an organization with 5 lines, I can assure you that 'B' will make a lot more money then 'A'. This is the beauty of an MLM business. It is fair, and bonuses are paid to people who work hard and for their leadership ability, not because they joined first.

   ii) From my twenty years of experience, I would advise people who are interested in MLM to avoid taking the risk of joining a new company, because the failure rate of new MLM companies is abnormally high. What is the use of being the first to join a new company, if there is a 90% probability that company will not be around next year?

e) I have no time
People who claim to have no time, are in fact telling you that they are not interested in the business, because of something else. To spend time, attacking lack of time, is a waste of time! Look for the real reason behind what they are saying. They may have a misconception as to what the business is all about, and think it is a pyramid scheme. They may think the business is not suitable for them because they

think it is door-to-door, or they do not understand the rewards in the marketing plan, and therefore do not see why they must give up free time to do the business. Maybe, they have no need for the business. Or then again, it may be their fear of failure or rejection. Maybe they have young children or sick parents at home that they have to consider. Maybe the reason is as simple as, not even having yet seen the marketing plan.

To start giving them a lecture and jumping to the wrong conclusion, is the wrong approach. Try the following to solve this objection:

i)   "I understand but since I am already here, would you give me half-an-hour of your time, to let me show you our marketing plan; can I do that for you?"

ii) "Great, I used to think like you, because I also thought that MLM was a door-to-door business. Let me very quickly show you the wholesale side of the business. I think you will be excited about it too."

iii) "Over the years, I have come to realize that those who tell me they have no time, normally have reasons other than time. As a friend, I will be more then happy to hear your real concern, and I want you to be frank with me. You will do that for me, won't you?"

iv) For people whose genuine concern is time, perhaps because they already have very busy lives, emphasize the royalty income part of the marketing plan, and how eventually, because of the business, they can gain their freedom.

f) I am not a good speaker
   Many people have low self-esteem, and public speaking is also a common fear. Sometimes, even the rich and powerful have this same fear, so when you answer this objection, make sure you really care.

i) "When we get involved in a new venture, it is only natural to not know what to say or speak about on the subject, simply because we do not yet understand the business, or have not accumulated enough knowledge. So this is only a temporary worry, don't you agree?"

ii) "I have got great news for you. In MLM, we insist that all new distributors use the ABC rule, and this will solve your challenge, won't it?"

iii) "Just sincerely sharing your excitement is more important and most powerful."

g) I have no friends

Again, the problem may not really be because they have no friends, but rather, that they are not interested in the business because of something else. I would advise going back into the marketing plan, to show them the benefits this business can bring to them, their family and friends.

If they have already seen the plan, but are still sincerely worried on this issue, you may want to go through their possible prospects with them:

Possible prospects:

1. family	7. store owners	13. travel agent
2. club members	8. teachers	14. postal deliverer
3. bankers	9. colleagues	15. classmates
4. your dentist	10. neighbors	16. your barber
5. church members	11. relatives	17. former office mates
6. your doctor	12. friends	18. people you respect

h) Products are too expensive

i) "Yes, I do understand your concern. Because of the bad image created by some pyramid schemes, it is normal for many people to think that all products sold through MLM companies are over-priced. However, let me assure you, that for a good MLM company like ours to be solid and long term, we have to price our products fairly, and actually, you will find that as a distributor you will be able to buy the products at below market value."

ii) "One of the things we are very proud of is that we offer our customers value for money, and over the last xxx years, we have been able to grow in leaps and bounds, because our customers appreciate us too. While some other products may seem cheap, the most important thing a consumer should consider, is value for money. While we can buy a laptop computer for, say, US$1,000, how come many of us choose to buy a laptop that costs US$2,000 to US$3,000? Value for money."

However, you must avoid criticizing the products or services your customers are currently using, because there is no way of knowing how strongly they believe in them, or because you cause them embarrassment in making them admit to having made a mistake in their original purchase.

i) I have no interest

For prospects who have not yet seen the plan:

"I appreciate your sincerity with me about MLM, and I do understand that many people have a misconception about this business. Since I am already here, can I ask you a favor as a friend? Would you give me an hour of your time, and let me show you our marketing plan. I promise you, I will not force you to join this business, if you do not like what you see. By the way, do feel free to stop me and ask any questions at any time. Is that okay with you?"

For those who have already seen the plan:

"I am happy that you are so sincere with me, and I want you to know that I make it a policy in MLM, never to force the business on my friends. All I ask is the opportunity to let me show you the business, and I really appreciate the time you give me. However, to help me improve myself, I would appreciate it if you will be frank with me, as to which part of the business you do not like."

or

"If you are not interested, will you be my customer, or can you introduce me to anyone who you think may be interested in the business?"

5. Conclusion:

Answering objections is based on learning, your belief level, confidence, and the accumulation of experience. However, it is very important that you listen to your prospects carefully, and understand the questions or objections they put to you, or you may end up coming to the wrong conclusions, giving the wrong answers, and they will end up wondering why you gave such stupid answers!

Story: Three old pilots

Three old pilots are walking on the ramp.
First one says, "Windy, isn't it?"
Second one says, "No, it's Thursday!"
Third one says, "So am I. Let's go get a beer."

Outline for Lesson 10
Answering objections

1. Introduction

a) Expect questions and even objections.

b) Be prepared and practice.

2. Attitude and skill

a) Listen and digest questions.

Story: Moishe

b) Do not exaggerate and be sincere.

c) It is a two-way communication.

d) Always first accept their objections, and then give your proper answers.

e) Have the habit of using a "tie-down" at the end of your answer.

Isn't it?	Wasn't it?	Don't we?
Aren't they?	Isn't it true?	Won't they?
Haven't they?	Won't you?	Don't you agree?

3. Teach down

a) You can increase your sales by sponsoring more new distributors, or improving the selling skills.

b) You can increase your sales by more hours and getting more customers, or improving your selling skills.

c) You can get distributors to stay in your organization by improving your communication skills.

4. Questions and objections to expect

a) Is it a pyramid scheme?

b) Market saturation.

c) Do I have to sell?

d) This business enriches the people who join at the ground floor.

e) I have no time.

f) I am not a good speaker.

g) I have no friends.

h) Products are too expensive.

i) I have no interest.

5. Conclusion

Answering objections is based on learning, your belief level, confidence and the accumulation of experience.

Story: Three old pilots

Lesson 11
'Playing games'

1. Introduction

Story: Hot Dog

A Chinese man visiting the United States for the first time, was feeling hungry after arriving at the airport. He entered a restaurant and the waitress gave him a menu. He looked at it and did not know what to order, as the Western food on the menu was foreign to him. He then noticed an item that interested him, Hot Dog. Being Chinese, he had eaten dog meat before, so he ordered a hot dog. When the hot dog arrived, he was horrified and told the waitress, "No, no, no, not this part of the dog."

There are many people today who need a business opportunity or second income, and it is so sad that on many occasions when we want to share the MLM opportunity with them, they want nothing to do with "this part of the dog", because of bad pyramid schemes, unscrupulous owners of these companies or unethical distributors.

2. Bad distributors can make legitimate companies into Pyramid schemes

Pyramid schemes are bad for our industry, but when distributors from legitimate companies also operate their business like pyramid schemes, playing the money game, ask yourself what the difference is between them and us? MLM is not a get-rich-quick scheme and was never designed to be one. All distributors must take the responsibility to work their business on proper MLM principles, and I hope you make the decision to build yours properly.

3. Good distributors under bad leaders

It is a sad fact that there are groups of distributors who love MLM, but do not understand what MLM is and how it should be done, simply because they are under bad leaders. Bad pyramid concepts and attitudes are just like 'letting the bad genie out of the magic lamp' and it is very difficult to stop, even when the leader realizes the mistakes they have made.

To this group of leaders or future leaders, I hope this book is of some help to you. Learn as much as you can, since you love this industry and have decided to make it the vehicle for achieving your dreams. Let us work together and I hope you will be one of our shining stars, a proud ambassador representing us in this great industry.

4. Those who are a force for bad

In any country or place of business, there is always a minority group of bad people who display a 'one-foot-in-jail and one-foot-outside-of-jail' attitude. They choose to have a criminal mind and be a force for bad, and their natural instincts are always to look for loopholes, and to walk down the wrong path. To this group, I would like to share another story.

Story: The frog and the centipede

One day, a centipede wanting to cross a stream asked a frog for help, because he could not swim. The frog refused, because the poisonous centipede might bite and kill him. The centipede replied, "I am not that stupid. If I bite you and you die, I will also drown, because I cannot swim." The frog thought about it, and finally agreed to help.

So the centipede climbed on the frog's back, and half way cross the stream, the frog felt a bite on his neck. The centipede had bitten him and as the frog was dying and the centipede drowning, the frog asked the centipede why. The centipede replied, "It is my natural instinct."

To this group, I want you to know that as a human being and not a centipede, you can make a decision to change your identity, to be a better person, and you can do it in a heartbeat. Do it for yourself, because I know you do not like who you are today. You were not born this way, but have just accumulated bad habits and made wrong decisions, and what was done, can be undone. Not only should you change for yourself, but also, if you have them, for your parents, your spouse or partner, and your children. What sort of example are you showing them, going through your life, deciding to do bad things all the time, on the basis that you decided to be a bad person? When you buy a computer, it comes with a manual but when a child is born, there is no manual and the child only has parents. Change now, it's just a decision.

5. 'Type A' person

While the above deals with bad people, I would also like to consider another group, containing 'Type A' people. This is where a person grows up in an environment that demands conditional love. Let me give you a couple of examples of conditional love. "Mummy will love you, if you eat your spinach." "Daddy will take you to the zoo on Sunday, if you do your homework." Conditions are always attached to love or any reward given and as a result, the person grows up doing things, not just because work has to be done, but rather in order to please others. They work as if they have a spear behind their back and are always under pressure to please others, to save face, to show off, or compete with others, when they have a goal to achieve.

There is nothing wrong to being a 'Type A' person, as many become great achievers, but I bring this subject up in this Lesson on 'playing games', because some leaders who are 'Type A' personalities, tend to 'play games' in our business. With the recognition, the pins, the travel incentives and other rewards given in most companies, a 'Type A' person will be under too much pressure to compete with others, and one of the easiest routes to take, is to 'play games'.

6. How to identify a 'Type A' person

a) The very first thing to be aware of, is that a 'Type A' who will never admit that they are a 'Type A'. So are you a 'Type A' person?

b) 'Type A' people are always too busy, and cannot slow down because they are afraid others may catch up with them. They never have enough time.

c) They put a lot of emphasis on title. A title may be more important than a salary increase or bonus.

d) They are unwilling to accept responsibility when thing go wrong, but are very fast in claiming all honors for the work of their followers.

e) They fear competition from their followers, and as a result, have difficulty in delegating work and responsibility.

f) They do not care who they step on when they climb the ladder of success, and as a result, they seldom climb to the very top, because others will pull them down. They climb very fast at the beginning, and their employer may be very impressed at this stage, but after some time, will begin to see the real results. They also have the tendency to sweep things under the carpet when no one is looking.

g) They get bothered when someone overtakes them on the highway.

7. What are the bad results of 'playing games'?

a) First and foremost, there will be financial loss to the downlines, as 'playing games' always involves the excessive buying of products to make pin levels, or to qualify for undeserved bonuses. Guess who gets the pin or the undeserved bonuses? Now guess who ends up with excess products, and also paid for them?

b) Second, there will be financial loss to the company, unless of course the company is an irresponsible pyramid scheme. All good MLM companies will try and buy back as much of the products as possible, to limit the damage already done or having to face serious price cutting.

c) Third, I can also guarantee you one thing. When any company has a

154

serious problem with price-cutting, it is because of the leaders 'playing games'. Distributors then get stuck with unsold products that they are desperate to unload, and the easiest way to get rid of them, is to sell them cheap. Some uplines have even been known to ask their downlines to buy from them, and not from the company, by offering prices below wholesale.

d) Fourth, and potentially the most damaging, is the effect it has on good leaders who are doing the business properly. Distributors 'playing games' are like unlawful drivers who drive on the hard shoulder during a traffic jam on a busy highway. They zoom past at high speed, while the rest of the people are stuck on the highway. When people 'play games' in MLM, they attain pin levels very quickly, even with a small group. Of course, they will also immediately have bigger bonus checks, since their group is throwing in their money to buy up products and create the false sales volume. The good leaders working the business properly, will be sitting there stuck in traffic, since in doing the business properly, they need time for the group to grow, before they see the good healthy sales result. However, when these good leaders are in the driver seat, we must not forget that they also have a bunch of passengers (downlines) in the car. These inexperienced downlines will begin to question the good leader and blame them for the slow progress. These downlines may think that the correct teachings of the good leader are 'wrong'. Some will even begin to believe they have joined the wrong group, and with the encouragement of bad leaders in bad groups, they may even change distributorship, using other people's names to re-register.

e) Fifth, 'playing games' will lead to fast but temporary inflated incomes, and when the bubble bursts, just like it does in an unhealthy stock market, those who made money will have difficulty in adjusting to the new reality. It is especially damaging when these leaders have bought high priced items, like a house or expensive cars on bank loans.

8. How to detect 'game playing'

a) When the group or upline recommend certain amounts of product loading to distributors, often in the region of US$1,000 to US$3,000.

b) When an upline encourages the downline to make certain pin levels or to buy certain amounts of products in a short time period, even though the downline does not have an organization to support that volume level or that amount of products.

c) Whenever a downline is asked to make a certain pin level or to buy certain amounts of product, which results in the upline moving up to another new pin level.

d) Whenever a downline is asked to make a certain pin level or to buy certain amounts of product, to qualify for a profit sharing program or for the upline to qualify for a certain incentive.

e) When downlines return products in large quantities or return cases of unopened products, and not by individual bottle or container, as would normally occur where a customers was returning product because of dissatisfaction.

9. Solution

a) Work the business at a healthy pace and the bonus you receive must reflect the number of distributors you have in your organization, which must also be equal to your leadership ability. There is no better solution, than where the leaders in a company decide to do the business properly, and on proper MLM principles.

b) I always teach downlines to listen to uplines, except in instances where a distributor feels that 'playing games' is going on and they are consequently feeling used, in which event they should feel free to question the motive of the upline. Keep it simple and ask that upline four questions, but all together, not one question at a time. Just say,

"Upline, I would like to ask you four questions."

"Why are you asking me to buy so many products or make the pin level?"

"How will this benefit me?"

"And how will this benefit you?"

"And is this the proper way to do the business?"

Then sit back, look into their eyes and listen. Normally the answer will be very short, something like, "Forget that I asked you."

c) Another very important solution to this problem, is for those leaders who have gone astray, to know and admit to their mistakes, and decide to change. In our business, it is all right to make mistakes, but it is not all right to continue making the mistake, and to refuse to change.

d) All good MLM companies have a 25/75 or 20/80 product-buying rule, insisting that unless a distributor has sold 75% to 80% of the products they have already bought, then they should not be ordering any more new products.

e) The very final solution, is the disciplining or termination of a leader. This is the last thing that any company wants to do, but all companies must also be aware that they are really the only final authority able to stop 'game playing'. A good leader cannot go to a crossline who has gone astray and try and stop it. Even an upline will find it difficult to stop a downline who has gone astray. So all companies must know that excessive 'game playing' and price-cutting, reflects on weak or bad management. It is a love-hate situation. They love the business volume and the money they make, but at the same time, hate the 'game playing' that is going on and therefore make a wrong decision, not to stop the nonsense. So I will conclude this chapter, by telling all companies, that the final blame always rests with the company. No need to point fingers elsewhere. Do you sincerely want to arrest the problem? If you do, you have to terminate or suspend (if your company has such a clause in your policy) a few distributorships, starting with the highest pin level leader responsible for causing the damage. Do not punish the mid level or lower level leaders, but start from the top.

Please read this lesson again.

Outline for Lesson 11
'Playing games'

1. Introduction

   Story: Hot dog

2. Bad distributors can make legitimate companies into Pyramid schemes

3. Good distributors under bad leaders

4. Those who are a force for bad

   Story: The frog and the centipede

5. 'Type A' person

6. How to identify a 'Type A' person
   a) 'Type A' will never admit they are 'Type A'.
   b) 'Type A' are always too busy. They never have enough time.
   c) The put a lot of emphasis on title.
   d) They are unwilling to assume responsibility.
   e) They fear competition from followers.
   f) They do not care who they step on when they climb the ladder of success.
   g) They get bothered when someone overtakes them on the highway.

7. What are the bad results of 'playing games'?

a) Financial loss to the downlines.
b) Second, there will be financial loss to the company.
c) Price-cutting.
d) Driving on the hard shoulder effect.
e) When the bubble bursts.

8. How to detect 'game playing'

a) When the group or upline recommends buying-in when joining.
b) Buying pin levels or certain amounts of products in a short period of time.
c) Buying pin levels or certain amounts of product to help the upline.
d) Buying pin levels or certain amounts of product for certain incentives.
e) Distributors return products in large quantities. Unopened cases.

9. Solution

a) Decide to do the business properly and on proper MLM principles
b) Question the motives of the upline. Ask four questions together:
   "Why are you asking me to buy so many products or make the pin level?"
   "How will this benefit me?"
   "And how will this benefit you?"
   "And is this the proper way to do the business?"
c) Must admit mistakes and decide to change.
d) MLM companies must have a 25/75 or 20/80 product buying rule.
e) The very final solution is the disciplining or termination of a leader.

Please read this lesson again.

Lesson 12
Goal setting

1. Introduction

87% of people do not set goals, because:
   a) They do not understand the importance of setting goals.
   b) They do not know how.
   c) They refuse to set goals because they fear failure and rejection.

Only the very low figure of 13% of people set goals but do you know that, if written down, 80% of those goals will materialize! If you know that and if you do the same, and 80% of your goals materialize, why not make a decision today to have the habit of setting goals? I believe you should.

Most people will surely have heard one or more of the following:
   a) A man without a goal, is like a ship without a rudder.
   b) A driver on the highway will not know where to go or when to stop, if they have no intended destination.
   c) A man goes bowling with the goal to strike down the ten pins but without those pins, he has no reason to go at all.
   d) A golfer takes a swing at the golf ball with the goal of hitting it on the fairway or the green, and eventually into the hole.

Do you really need any more examples to convince yourself that goal setting is important? If you do, then I think you are on the brink of being unteachable, and you are probably wasting your time reading my book. So please, set goals.

2. There are five things that will influence or affect our lives

a) Our environment

For example, the country and community we live in, the economy, the traffic etc. Do you think your life would be different, if you were born in communist Cuba or North Korea, instead of the United States of America? Do you think the economy would affect your life, if you were a young man looking for work during the Great Depression in the 1930's?

b) Events

These can be natural, international, or personal events. Do you think that for a healthy person who suffers an accident and is now a cripple, the event changed his/her life? Do you think the Second World War affected the lives of many during that era? Think about the day when your sponsor showed you the MLM opportunity, and how it has changed your life today. If not for that event, you probably would not even read this book.

c) Knowledge

Education plays a very important part in our lives. It affects our lifestyle, and even influences the way we talk. Let me tell you for sure, people who are not involved in MLM, think we talk funny! Words like 'uplines' and 'downlines' are not even in the dictionary. We use terms like 'breaking a certain number of legs' to move up to pin levels. People who do not understand our business, may think we are a bunch of gangsters, going around with the goal to break legs.

Do you think the education of a doctor also affected his income and lifestyle? You bet.

d) Past results

Past results will also affect our lives. We often hear of criminals as having come from troubled pasts, and at the same time, many successful people give credit to their ancestors, their parents, or even their grandparents, as the reason for their success. People tell others, "That is how I have always done things." We hear of people talking about their past girlfriends or boyfriends, who are now someone else's wife or husband. While it is good to hold on to sweet memories, and learn from past mistakes, past results are yesterday and yesterday is gone; we have to look forward to tomorrow.

e) Results in advance

When we talk about goal setting, we are going to focus on the fifth thing that influences our lives, that is, the results in advance. The dreams and hopes as to what we may achieve or become, the wealth we may accumulate or attain or other benefits, will also influence our life. By the way, the opposite and negative effect is just as powerful; believing that we will fail and that those things are unattainable. Yes, the result in advance or the future will also affect our life.

3. The rule governing goal setting

Potential + Action = Results = Attitude

Let us study this rule and these four powerful words.

Example one

You are working for a very wealthy man, who only pays you US$2,000 (Result) a month (this may be a very good income in most countries but a very poor income for Americans living in the United States). You have to work five days a week, eight hours a day. How will the result, which is the US$2,000 a month, affect your attitude? I bet your attitude is not very good. How will this attitude, in turn, affect your action and your potential? So for many people, their life is governed by the rule, that is:

Result = Attitude = Action + Potential

Note the important word, Result.

Example two

Story: Young man who saw the result in advance

A young man is in love with a beautiful lady, who is also very much in love with him. However, there is a problem. The lady is the daughter of a very wealthy man, and the young man is only a schoolteacher who makes a petty salary of only US$4,000 a month. As a result, the parents of the lady objected to the relationship, which is understandable in view of the fact that some of her evening dresses cost over US$4,000!

One day, this young man is shown our great MLM business. He sees the potential of the opportunity, and begins to dream about the result he may be able to achieve. He begins to dream of being a very successful leader and of his ability to make over US$20,000 a month, get acceptance from the girl's parents and marry her. How will this possible result in advance affect his attitude? How will this attitude in turn affect his actions, and how will these actions in turn make use of his potential. So for you, or anyone interested in success, especially in the accumulation of wealth and in goal setting, the rule should be:

Result in advance = Attitude = Action +

Potential

Having been in the business for over 20 years, I have come across many distributors who make all kinds of excuses as to why they cannot attend certain meetings or trainings. I have heard of ridiculous ones, like because it is winter, it is too cold, or it is summer and it is too hot. By the way, what is the right temperature to attend events or meetings, when it is neither too cold nor too hot? Do you think this young man will have these problems? It is therefore very important for all sponsors to help their downlines see the benefits or result in advance, and the pleasure they will gain from being successful in their new MLM adventure. In the great book, "Jonathan Seagull" by Richard Bach, there is a part I really like. It reads, "You must begin by knowing that you have already arrived."

4. The conscious and the subconscious mind

Goal setting boils down to a person's ability to see what they want in the future and taking action, using the potential within them to achieve it. When we talk about using one's potential, a lesson on goal setting will never be truly complete unless we spend some time talking about our conscious and subconscious mind, and the hidden potential within us. Our mind is like an iceberg, where only 10% or our conscious mind is above water and the remaining 90%, our subconscious mind, is below the water. Experts tell us that we hardly use 10% of our mind and that if we can harness the power of our subconscious mind, we can achieve great things and 'move mountains', since it represents the biggest mass of the iceberg.

Story: The Captain and the Laborer

To emphasize on this point, I love to refer to the conscious mind as the captain of a steamboat and the subconscious mind as the laborer whose job is to shovel coal into the burner that powers the boat. The captain, representing the conscious mind, has total control of his five senses. When he sees all is clear, he gives the order for full-steam-ahead. The man who shovels coal, the subconscious mind, cannot see what the captain sees but he will listen to the captain's order, and start to shovel coal into the burner that powers the boat.

It is of the utmost importance for anyone who is interested in success, to always be positive and talk positively, which can be controlled using our conscious mind; and when the subconscious mind begins to blindly believe the conscious mind, things will happen. On the other hand, when distributors do not know how to master their emotions, and begin to consciously send negative messages to the subconscious mind, the results will be negative. Do not waste time indulging in negative, self-fulfilling prophecy. By the way, I have no problem if you indulge in positive, self-fulfilling prophesy.

5. Watch your Language

A good place to start, will be to control your language, and language is connected to your focus and belief. When a person thinks a task is too difficult, their natural language is, "It is too difficult." Many things in life are difficult, but difficulties do not mean they cannot be done. If they are important enough, we can always find ways to solve these challenges. What do you think will happen, if you use your conscious mind and continue to send the message that you believe something is too difficult and cannot be done? Will the laborer continue to shovel coal into the burner, or stop working?

Train your 'Captain' to say the right things, until the 'Laborer' believes. Decide for yourself, whether you want your 'Laborer' to believe things that are going to help you progress, or things to pull you down. Both are just as powerful. Please do not under-estimate the power of your potential and your subconscious mind.

I once attended a training program by the great master, Anthony Robbins, and in the training, there was a fire walk. All students were trained to say, "Yes, I can." and to think of the fire as cool moss. To walk from the training room to the fire walk, was about one kilometer, and by the time they arrive at the fire pit, the students had said, "Yes, I can and cool moss" about 100 times. Over 1,000 students walked across over forty feet of burning coal, and not a single student got burnt!

Can you imagine going through life saying, "It is too difficult," "I can't," "I am too tired," and all the other negatives, until they became negative incantations, simply because you did not control your negative emotions? Make a decision, today, to learn a new set of positive language statements, such as, "I can," "No problem," "Considered it done," "I am good at what I do," "I am tough," "Outstanding," "Well done" and "Marvelous," creating positive incantations for yourself. Control the 'Captain', to send the right message to the 'Laborer', so that you can use the potential hidden in you.

166

Story: Two men went to the Pub

Two men went drinking one night and they had quite a few. At mid-night, the first man decided to 'call it a night', as he had promised his wife to be home by twelve. The second man decided to continue drinking.

The first man decided to take a shortcut through a cemetery, and he fell into a hole dug for a potential customer. Not wanting to spend the night there, he tried to climb out but failed. He shouted for help but there was nobody around to help, so he gave up and went to sleep in a corner.

At 2.00am, the second man also had to leave when the bar closed. He too decided to take the shortcut through the cemetery and like-wise, he also fell into the hole. He tried to climb out but failed, for he had drunk even more. He shouted for help and woke up the first man.

The first man, seeing his friend jumping and shouting for help, said, "You will never get out of here." The second man discovered his potential and got out real quick!

6. Psycho-cybernetics

What this means is to keep on doing things with your conscious mind, until your subconscious mind takes over. Let me give you an example. Do you still remember the first time you learned how to ride a bicycle? How difficult it was learning the task of balancing yourself on a machine that had only two wheels. The number of times you fell over and hurt yourself. You kept on practicing, until you knew how. Once you know how, you can just jump on one and easily find your balance. You do not even think about it. How come? The bike still has only two wheels? It is because you are now using your subconscious mind. The same goes with learning how to dance, or how to drive a car.

As you take your new venture into the world of MLM, there will be many new things that you have never done before and find difficult. Do not give up. Keep on practicing until your subconscious mind takes over and when you attain that level, it will just be as easy as riding a bicycle. Do things until your subconscious mind takes over, and everything will be easy.

Workshop: Goal Setting

a) What do you want in the next 10 years? Goals must be realistic and attainable. Time: 15 minutes.

_____

_____

_____

_____

_____

_____

_____

_____

_____

_____

_____

_____

_____

_____

The following questions should help:
1) What do you want to do/see?
2) Where do you want to go?
3) What do you want to have?
4) What do you want to share?
5) What do you want to be?

b) Put a time on your goals/dreams. Time: 3 min.

c) Select the 4 most important one-year goals and write a few words as to why you think they are important. Time: 10 min.

_____
_____
_____
_____
_____
_____
_____
_____
_____
_____
_____
_____
_____
_____
_____
_____

d) What do you feel? Comfortable, uncomfortable, unsure, not as important as you initially thought, or you must have it.

_____
_____
_____
_____
_____
_____
_____
_____

e) If you are given US$10 million today, what changes will you make in your life? Will you still work where you working now? Time: 2 min.

_____

_____

_____

_____

_____

_____

_____

_____

f) What are you thinking of doing, but dare not? Time: 1min

_____

_____

_____

_____

_____

_____

_____

g) What would you do, if you have only 6 months to live?

_____

_____

_____

_____

_____

_____

_____

_____

Are your four most important one-year goals still that important?

h) When are you most proud of yourself?

_____

_____

_____

_____

_____

_____

_____

_____

i) If you knew that you cannot fail, what would you like to do?

_____

_____

_____

_____

_____

_____

7. Dream Board

The last thing I want you to do to close this Lesson, is to make yourself your Dream Board, to help you clearly visualize what you want, and this will automatically send messages to your subconscious mind. This is probably the most important thing you must now do for this topic to be effective, and the bad news is that over 50% of the people will not do it. In the very beginning of this Lesson, I told you, "If written down, 80% of goals set by them will materialize." So please, you must go home and design your Dream Board. Buy a piece or two of Styrofoam, which you can get it from any good stationary shop at a cost of under US$1. Put up your Dream Board using a double-sided tape, preferably in a place where those people who do not believe you, cannot see it. From this Workshop, you should already have a fair amount of information for your Dream Board. A suggestion will be to divide your Dream Board into the following categories:

a) Business goals for your MLM business

Since this is a goal setting training for your MLM business, the very first thing I would like you to do is to set your MLM business goals. For example, when would you like to achieve certain levels in the marketing plan? How many prospects will you show the business to in a week? What sales volume do you want to have each month? How many meetings and trainings do you need to attend a week or a month? How many times should you call your upline in a week or a day?

I cannot over-emphasize enough the importance of having very clear weekly and daily goals for this section. How many days a week do you want to do the business? What days? What time? For those who are full-time in the business, I want your daily and weekly goals to be very detailed, especially your daily goals. I want you to write down what time you need to wake up in the morning, what time for lunch and dinner, and what time you need to go to bed, and a detailed schedule as to what you do in between.

b) Your personal improvement goals

For example, how many books you would like to read a month? How much weight you would like to lose and the time taken to lose it?

c) Your financial goals

How much money you would like to have in the bank? How much would you like to save every month? If you want US$100,000 in the bank five years from now, but you are only saving US$100 a month due to your present low income, you know that you will not be able to achieve this goal. However, please do not give up on your goal. Start to find solutions to make more money, to make this goal attainable. Do not under-estimate your potential and your subconscious mind.

d) Material things

This is probably the most superficial, but also the most fun thing in goal setting; to see the material things you can acquire if you have financial wealth. What car would you like to drive? What color? A nice home or homes? Diamonds? Nice clothes? Cut pictures out from magazines and brochures of the things you would like, and put them on your Dream Board. When you achieve certain goals and have the money, do reward yourself. I have observed several shows performed in Marine Parks, where they get dolphins and seals to perform feats. You will notice that when the feats are being performed, the animals will get a reward. It works on the same principle with humans. We must desire certain things and also reward ourselves. We must have a reason why we do what we do, and then reward ourselves, so that we understand why we spend late nights, give meetings, follow up, retail, customer service, etc.

e) Social goals

Give something back to the community, your town, your club, your Church/Temple/Mosque, your country.

f) Family goals

One of the strongest driving forces to get us to achieve is love for family. For your spouse, children, parents, in-laws etc. What would you like to do or get for them?

g) Your spiritual goals

If you are religious.

Points to note

a) Design realistic and exciting goals.

b) Aim higher.

c) Put dates on your goals.

d) Your goals should be divided into:

   i) Short-term.

   ii) Mid-term.

   iii) Long-term goals.

e) Visualize your goals and read them three times a day.

f) Bravely tell your uplines and business associates about your goals. Do not under estimate the power of words. Try this:

   i) Ask the biggest man in the audience to stand up and ask him how heavy he is (not ladies please, for obvious reasons).

   ii) Now ask him to sit down. Have you observed how many pounds you have moved with your words?

8. Conclusion:

I would like to conclude this Lesson with the great speech given by Sir Winston Churchill, made on 29 October, 1941, to the boys at Churchill's old public [private] school, Harrow. This is to remind you to expect challenges when you want better things and a better lifestyle. There is a price to be paid if you want good things in life, and when you are faced with these challenges, please never give in.

Story: "Never give in" by Sir Winston Churchill

"Never give in--never, never, never, never, in nothing great or small, large or petty, never give in, except to convictions of honor and good sense. Never yield to force; never yield to the apparently overwhelming might of the enemy."

He then walked away to a standing ovation.

Outline for Lesson 12
Goal setting

1. Introduction

Fact. 87% (Do not) = 13% (Do) = 80% (Goals will materialize)

2. There are five things that will influence or affect our lives

a) Our environment

The country, community, economy, traffic, etc.

Born in communist Cuba or North Korea vs. United States of America?

The Great Depression in the 1930's?

b) Events

Natural, International or Personal events.

A healthy person after an accident who is now a cripple.

The Second World War.

Being sponsored into MLM opportunity.

c) Knowledge

Education affects our lifestyle/way we talk.

People not in MLM, think we talk funny.

Education of a doctor, also affected his income and lifestyle?

d) Past Results

Criminals coming from troubled past.

Successful people giving credit to their ancestors, parent, grandparents.

How they have always done things.

Past girlfriends or boyfriends.

Past results are yesterday. Look forward to tomorrow.

e) Results in advance

What we may achieve or become.

The wealth we may accumulate
The opposite and negative effect is just as powerful.

3. The rule governing goal setting

Potential + Action = Results = Attitude

Example one

Working for a very wealthy man pays you US$2,000 a month. Work five days a week, eight hours a day

Result = Attitude = Action + Potential

Example two

Story: Young man who saw result in advance

A young man is in love with a beautiful lady.
Saw the potential of the business = over US$20,000 a month.

Result in advance = Attitude = Action + Potential

Distributors make all kinds of excuses, why they cannot attend certain meetings or trainings. Example: Winter too cold or summer too hot. What is the right temperature?
Important for all sponsors to help their downlines see the benefits or result in advance.

"Jonathan Seagull" by Richard Bach "You must begin by knowing that you
have already arrived."

4. The Conscious and the Subconscious mind

Our mind is like an iceberg. 10% conscious mind above water and 90% subconscious below the water.
Experts tell us that we hardly use 10% of our mind.

Story: The Captain and the Laborer

Conscious mind as the captain. Has total control of his five senses
Subconscious mind as the laborer. Cannot see but he will listen to orders.

5. Watch your Language

Our language is also connected to our focus and belief.
Send negative message and the laborer will stop working.

Story. Two men went to the Pub

6. Psycho-cybernetics

Keep doing things with your conscious mind until your subconscious mind takes over.

Examples:
  Ride a bicycle
  How to dance
  How to drive a car

Workshop: On Goal Setting

7. Dream Board

8. Conclusion

Story: Sir Winston Churchill, "Never give in."

Lesson 13
How to conduct a one-to-one OPP

1. Introduction

One of the most important skills you must possess to become successful in MLM, is the ability to present the marketing plan. All distributors must start to learn, and then present, the one-to-one OPP as soon as possible. This is easy, once you accept that this is something you have to do as part of your occupation in MLM; just like learning how to use a computer is part of the occupation of a secretary. It is not an option, and having decided, the goal is to be able to present the marketing plan within two weeks of starting in MLM. This goal and desire will translate into making efforts to listen and learn from top leaders for the following fourteen days.

2. Purpose

a) It is important that all distributors learn how to do their own OPP, so that they can be more independent in the expansion of their business. No sponsor or upline can be available at all times, and when downlines do not know how to present the marketing plan themselves, it slows the expansion of the organization.

b) Distributors cannot just wait for the big presentation of the OPP to a large audience, normally taking place during an evening, since that may not be convenient to some prospects. They may live very far away from the venue, have young children at home, or a thousand other reasons. So when distributors know how to do the one-to-one OPP, the business becomes so portable, you can even give a presentation during your holiday in Hawaii!

c) All sponsors must help their new distributors, to in-turn sponsor their prospects at the first few opportunity meetings, using the ABC rule. If sponsors do not know how to do the one-to-one OPP, how can we apply the ABC rule?

d) In MLM, we can never under-estimate the power of duplication. We duplicate both right and wrong things. When a good upline shows by example, downlines copy. It is a monkey-see, monkey-do business. Any upline who does not know how to present a one-to-one OPP, will have a group who all do not know how to present the marketing plan, and a group like this will grow at a very slow pace.

3. What is OPP?

Before I go into how to do a one-to-one OPP presentation, I want first to ask you what an OPP is. You may think, "Why does Eddy ask me this stupid question, when we are nearly at the end of this book?" The reason is very simple. Over the years, I have seen all kinds of OPP's being presented, and many times I wondered whether what I saw was an OPP, or just a product presentation, or just small-talk, or just 'beating around the bush'.

My friends, let's get things clear. OPP stands for 'opportunity meeting' or 'opportunity presentation'. In the dictionary, the word opportunity means 'a chance to do something' and when we talk about an opportunity meeting or presentation, what we are really talking about is a meeting or presentation where the prospect is given a chance to go into business with us. Normally, people go into a business venture with you because of the compensation, and the products are just the vehicle to get that compensation.

Granted that it is also possible to sponsor people, just because we or our prospects get excited about certain products, but to do an OPP properly, prospects need to be shown how they can have a chance to go into business with us, with exciting products, to make some money, by presenting the marketing plan. So when I talk about an opportunity meeting or presentation, what I want you to do is to be able to present the marketing plan properly, so that when you are finished, your prospects see the benefits they will be able to get to satisfy their needs. Show the business, please. It is not a product presentation. Product presentation is just part of the OPP. Show them the marketing plan and SHOW THEM THE MONEY.

4. Time allocation for a one-to-one OPP

a) Opening: 5-10 minutes. After the handshake greeting and taking your seats, I would like you to spend only a little time on small-talk and then get down to business right away, especially if the prospect is someone you do not know well. We live in a busy world and your prospect may have a very tight schedule.

b) Marketing plan: 20 to 30 minutes. A good marketing plan takes some time to be presented, as nearly all companies pay out at least 5 to 6 kinds of bonuses:
   i) Retail profit.
   ii) Monthly bonus/override.
   iii) Leadership bonus.
   iv) Higher pin bonus.
   v) Profit sharing.
   vi) Travel or car incentives.

   You have to show at least the basic two, the Monthly bonus and the Leadership bonus, and these two bonuses take time.

c) Conclusion. When you have finished your presentation, let the situation takes its natural course.

5. Sell ideas

When you present your marketing plan, you must also sell ideas to go with these bonuses. The following are some of the ideas I sell when I present my OPP:

Idea 1 (Traditional business vs. MLM)

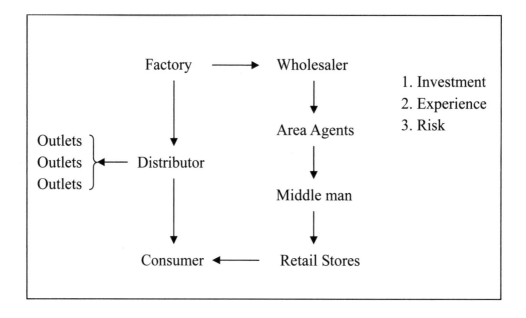

The points I emphasize here are:

a) MLM is like any traditional business where there is retail and wholesale business, and how we use the marketing plan in MLM to redistribute the same profits that are shared amongst traditional business merchants.

b) No investment or very little investment required.

c) No experience required. We will teach you how.

d) No risk.

Idea 2 (Law of Leverage)

This is my favorite. I have always believed that the multiplication of time through others, or the law of leverage, is the most important secret to wealth. This idea hits a 'home run' every time, as it is very easy to explain and understand, and at the same time, most of our prospects do not have a business of their own, and have no opportunity to multiply their time. Some prospects have little or no knowledge of this law, and when they see it and it hits home, they may realize that MLM is their only option. Here is how I show them:

There are only 24 hours in a day. When we minus the time we spend sleeping, eating, commuting to work, with the family, reading the newspaper, watching the TV, etc., we will normally be left with about 8 hours a day in which to make money. If we work 5 days a week and out of the 52 weeks in a year, we work 50 weeks and we work for 40 years in our lifetime, we will have 80,000 hours to make money in that lifetime.

8 hrs x 5 days = 40 hrs/week x 50 weeks x 40 years = 80,0000 hours

If we are paid US$30 per hour, we will be paid

80,000 x US$30 = US$2.4 million

If we only work with our own two hands, without multiplying our time, how can we ever be wealthy? Let's see how the rich make their money:

Bill Gates has got 40,000 people working for him and if everyone gives him 8 hours a day, he will have 320,000 hours per day.

40,000 x 8 hours = 320,000 hours per day.

If Mr. Gates only makes US$10 per hour, he will make

32,000 x US$10 = US$ 3.2 million per day.

However, statistics show that he makes more than that, as there are also tens-of-thousands of people who multiple time for him, but who are not directly under his pay role. Do you seriously think that Mr. Gates could be the richest man in the world, if he only used his own two hands to create his wealth? Do you think you will do well, if like most people you only use your own two hands?

Some numbers on Wal-Mart for your reference; How big would Wal-Mart be, if it was just a 'mom and pop convenience store', around the corner in your neighborhood?

They have over 100 million customers per week.

Sell over 150,000 products.

Have 356.67 million square feet of shopping area.

Employ over 1.3 million employees (1 million in the USA + 300,000 outside the USA).

Advertising budget for 2002 was US$676 million.

Their annual sales for 2002 were US$244 billion.

Net profit for 2002 was US$6.671 billion.

They paid US$4.48 billion in taxes.

Idea 3 (Royalty income or Leadership bonus)

When your downline also makes the leadership level, resulting in no more override bonus being payable, a leadership bonus kicks in. To me this is the most attractive part in the MLM business, and it motivated me into leaving my restaurant business 23 years ago. In most companies this income is also a royalty income that can be passed down to your family, just like the royalty incomes received by writers, singers, composers and inventors. For example: When Elvis Presley died, on August 18th, 1977, his net worth was less then US$10 million dollars but today his daughter Lisa Marie, is worth over US$100 million dollars, and this money is mostly from her father's royalty income. Elvis is still RCA's number one selling artist and his record sales had exceeded 1 billion by 1997.

Writers also get this special income. Ernest Hemingway wrote a few good books and later killed himself. His children became very wealthy people from the royalties on his books. Imagine if you had written the Bible - it's been the best seller for over a thousand years! Bill Gates also receives royalty incomes. He gets millions of dollars from computer companies who use his operating system. Imagine if you were the person who invented the cellular phone. Compare the royalty income paid by your MLM company to the royalty paid by many franchise stores like McDonalds, KFC, and Burger King, etc.

Remember; sell ideas when you sell your OPP.

6. Things to prepare

a) A good pen.
b) Writing paper/pad.
c) Your company manual, monthly magazine (especially if it contains meeting schedules) and other sales aids which your company produces.
d) Products for demo, brochures and samples.

7. Points to note

a) Coordinate your appointment time well between your prospect and you.
b) Choose a suitable location.
c) Pay attention to your prospect's reaction. Talk about their needs, not yours.
    Depending on your prospect, you may need to talk about your incentive programs or profit sharing.
d) Do not 'beat around the bush'.
e) Be honest and excited.
f) 100% memorize an OPP. Water boils at 100 degrees centigrade, not at 99 degrees. Your prospect may never give you a second chance.

8. What you must do after an OPP is over

a) Sign up prospect.
b) Leave some follow-up material and make next appointment.

9. Conclusion

Story: Roger Bannister

For thousands of years, no man had ever run one mile in under 4 minutes. Studies were made and scientific explanations given as to why a man could not run that fast. Some of the reasons were:

a) Man has only two legs and most animals have four; therefore we cannot run that fast.
b) Man has too much body fat when compared to most animals.
c) Man runs upright and wind resistance makes it impossible to run that fast.
d) The leg bones and muscles of man are not built to run so fast.

On the 6th May 1954, Roger Bannister broke the '4 minute mile' with the time of 3 minutes 59.4 seconds. The next year, 37 others also broke the '4-minute mile', yet for centuries no man had been able to run it in under 4 minutes. How was it, that after Roger Bannister broke the record, 37 others also did it the following year? The reason is that one man had showed it could be done and others believed. Be the Roger Bannister for your group. Lead by example.

On July 7th 1999, in Rome, Hicham El Guerrouj, a 24-year-old Moroccan, smashed the mile record in a time of 3 minutes 43.13 seconds. He beat Roger Bannister's time by 16.27 seconds. Since a mile is equal to 1609 meters, Hicham El Guerrouj ran at a speed of 7.211 meters per second and beating Roger Bannister's time by 16.27 seconds meant that he would also have beaten him by 117.32 meters! It is amazing, how once a set of beliefs are changed, what the human potential can achieve.

10. You must know how to teach down: Story: Two professors with different teaching systems

An experiment was done with two groups of students. They were divided into 2 classes, with two lecturers, and they were all given a 5-week course.

For Group A students:

The lecturer stood in front of the class and taught for four full weeks. They could just listen to his lectures, but not ask questions for the four weeks.

For Group B students:

For the 1st week the lecturer stood in front of the class and taught. The students could ask questions at any time.

For the 2nd week the lecturer asked the students to sit in a semi-circle, with no desks, and he stood in front of the class and taught. The students could ask questions at any time.

For the 3rd week he asked the class to sit in a full circle, and he sat with the students and taught. The students could ask questions and give their input at any time.

For the 4th week the lecturer again sat in the full circle, but the class was held discussion style and the lecturer could only ask the following questions:
    Any other questions?
    Does anyone have anything more to say or add?

On the first day of the fifth week, both lecturers reported that they were both too busy that day and could not come to class. Group A students all packed up after a few minutes and went home, but Group B students sat in the full circle and continued their discussion.

Observe carefully how I teach my new distributors

You will all know by now, that whenever I sponsor new distributors, I immediately apply the ABC rule and do not allow them to do at least the first 5 Opps to their prospects. The reason for this is that I want to teach them while I help them. They have to organize a weekly home meeting for me and this is what we do. For every step, I teach or go through what they will be saying or need to say.

For the first meeting, my new distributor's job is that of the host and is just to introduce me (I teach them how to welcome the guests, and how to introduce me). I then take over, show the marketing plan, do some product demonstration and do the close, help register those interested, answer questions and also help with any product orders.

For the second meeting, my new distributor's job again is to introduce me but after the marketing plan, they will be asked to give a testimony as to what they see in the business, why they are so excited and their dreams (again, I teach them or they have to tell me, what they may say).

For the third meeting, my new distributor's job again is to introduce me but after the marketing plan, they will be asked to talk about some products and do some demonstration (again, I teach them what they have to do and say. They must do the product demo for me first. We must be professional and there is no room for accidents). They have to play a more proactive part now, in registering those who are interested, answering questions, and helping with the product orders.

For the fourth meeting, I will take over the job of introducing the speaker, and my new distributor's job is to show the marketing plan (I always let them know from the very beginning, that they will have to do the Opp within two weeks. They may have to do a practice one for me first). I let the audience know it is the new distributor's first time and ask for their help and support. I will immediately take over if they need help, and I do the product part and the close. If they do not do a good job, I tell them it is normal, and always heap them with praise. No negatives please.

For the fifth meeting, I again do the job of introducing the

speaker, and my new distributor's job is to show the marketing plan. I pre-warn the host that from now on, I will begin to leave earlier, after the product demonstration and close, as their friends may be more comfortable with me not around. I try to be nearby having a coffee, just in case they need help, by calling my cell phone.

For the sixth to tenth meetings, I begin to play a lesser role

and sometimes I do not even show up. During this time, I look for and train new leaders under this group, and they then have to do the introduction, give a testimony, or do the product demonstration during our weekly home meeting, in order to help the upline.

At the same time, I will try to find a leader under this group, in order to start the above procedure all over again.

For the one-to-one OPP, you must be the 'Roger Bannister' of your group, for your downlines to duplicate. Lead by example and learn to do it in two weeks. This is an instruction, not an option.

Outline for Lesson 13
How to conduct a one-to-one OPP

1. Introduction

Something you have to do as part of your occupation.
Learn in two weeks. Do it immediately.

2. Purpose

a) Can be more independent.
   No sponsor or upline can be available at all times.
b) Cannot just wait for the big presentation of the OPP. May not be convenient to some prospects.
   The business becomes portable.
c) Help their new distributors using the ABC rule.
d) Power of duplication. We duplicate both right and wrong things.
   It is a monkey-see, monkey-do business.

3. What is OPP?

OPP stands for an opportunity meeting.
'Opportunity' means 'a chance to do something'
Present the marketing plan properly. Show the business please.

4. Time allocation for a one-to-one OPP

a) Opening: 5-10 min.
b) Marketing plan: 20 to 30 min.
c) Conclusion.

5. Sell ideas

Idea 1 (Traditional business vs. MLM)

Idea 2 (Law of Leverage)

Idea 3 (Royalty income or Leadership bonus.)

Remember; Sell ideas when you sell your OPP.

6. Things to prepare

7. Points to note

8. What you must do after an OPP is over?

9. Conclusion

Story: Roger Bannister

10. You must know how to teach down

Story: Two professors with different teaching systems

Observe carefully how I teach my distributors

Lesson 14
Positive thinking and Pleasure

1. Introduction

I would like to start this exercise by asking you if you think you are a happy person. If you think you are, do the muscles on your face know? We all know that MLM is a people business, and we must also be aware that people do not like to be around unhappy and miserable people. Bad people cannot be successful in our business and they do not deserve success for what they are, but the sad thing is that unhappy and miserable people are generally not bad people. They are just people who have a negative outlook on life, and I would love to see them do well in our business, but their negativity will turn people off and lead to their failure, or at best, very limited success.

So my friends, please choose to be a positive person, as it is a lot better than the alternative, which brings with it pain to your life and the lives of others around you. As a human being, we are like a pebble thrown into a pond or lake, and we create ripples. We need to ask ourselves at all times, whether we create happy ripples or unhappy ripples in the lake or pond we are in. Of course we are free to choose whether we want to be happy or not and it is nobody else's business, but if we choose to be unhappy and negative, we also need to ask ourselves how this effects others?

How does negativity effect:
>   My spouse and children?
>   My parents or in-laws?
>   My colleagues at work?
>   Business associates in my MLM business?

2. It is a state of mind, not the blessings you received

To be happy and positive, or unhappy and negative, is all in your state of mind. It is in your desire and ability to make intelligent and positive decisions to achieve that happy state, or the mistake of making unhealthy and negative decisions resulting in that unhappy state. What do you think Elvis Presley, Marilyn Monroe, Naomi Campbell, Prince Charles, Princess Diana, OJ Simpson, and Mike Tyson all have in common?

It is their ability to find pain in their lives, even though they are envied for the blessings they've received. Let me share with you two recent stories on this issue:

Leslie Cheung

On April 1 2003, Leslie Cheung, a famous 46-year-old Hong Kong singer and movie star, took his own life by jumping off the balcony of the 5 star Mandarin Oriental Hotel in Hong Kong, ending one of the more remarkable acting and performing careers in Asian entertainment history. He scrawled out a note before he jumped and "Depressed!" was the first sentence. At the time of his death, Cheung had reportedly amassed a personal fortune of US$67 million. It must be really depressing, to be so famous and have $67 million!

Carolyn Bessette

When Carolyn Bessette married John F. Kennedy Jr. on Cumberland Island, Ga., in 1996, she bagged for herself one of the most eligible bachelors in the world. Rich, famous and powerful. However, according to a new book by Edward Klein, 'The Kennedy Curse', the marriage of John F. Kennedy Jr. and his wife Carolyn Bessette Kennedy was foundering amid drug use and suspicions of adultery when the couple died in a plane crash in 1999. She was a highly-strung, unhappy, cocaine addict. He was frustrated and about to file for divorce.

Let me share with you two important secrets, if you want to be happy and positive:

   a) Heaven and hell is between your two ears.
   b) We are all born with two lives: the one we are born with, and the one that we can change.

In this exercise, we will deal with three things:

   a) The source or root, to positive and negative emotions.
   b) The five rules that govern these two kinds of emotions.
   c) The three keys to help us control negative emotions.

3. The source of positive and negative thinking

In the great book, 'Think and grow rich' by Napoleon Hill, it states that we have seven major positive and negative emotions. They are:

Positive	Negative
Desire	Fear
Faith	Jealousy
Love	Hatred
Sex	Revenge
Enthusiasm	Greed
Romance	Superstition
Hope	Anger

4. The five rules that govern our mind and the two kinds of emotions

Rule No. 1

Our mind functions automatically, whether you make any effort to influence it or not. It will not remain idle. Even when you are resting, playing golf, listening to a lecture, reading, driving, cooking, doing the laundry, when the boss is talking, whatever, it is quite normal to find your mind wandering and thinking about other things. Even when we are sleeping, the mind may still be in the wilderness.

Rule No. 2

Negative emotions will come voluntarily by themselves, whereas positive emotions have to be applied. If we use air to represent negative emotions, we all know that air will automatically occupy the vacuum of an empty glass. Let us use water, to represent positive emotions. Water has to be poured into the glass to fill it, since it will not go in automatically. The same applies with our mind. It is just like the glass. If we leave it empty, negative emotions will automatically come to fill that empty vacuum. Positive emotions, on the other hand, have to be injected. We have to train to pour water into the glass to fill it and effort is required.

Rule No. 3

Positive and negative emotions cannot occupy the mind at the same time. This is good news and a major key in controlling your negative emotions. When you fill the space taken by air with water, air can no longer take up that space. So my friend, train yourself to inject positive emotions into your mind and by making this into a habit, the result will be that when your mind is filled with positive emotions, you cannot be negative, even if you want to.

Rule No. 4

The most important thing I learnt from Anthony Robbins is, " Whether our positive or negative emotions bring for us pain or pleasure, everything we do in our lives is driven by our fundamental need to avoid pain, and our desire to gain pleasure." In the battle between pain and pleasure, pain will normally win. In other words, even if a person knows a job will give them the salary they need, that person may give up the job if they hate it. I repeat pain will normally win.

Rule No. 5

We can connect anything to pleasure or pain, by choice. If your grandfather passes away, you are the only heir named to his estate and in his Will, he leaves you a fortune of US$10 million cash, what will your feeling be? Obviously sorrow at the death of your grandfather, but what would you like to do with the money? You may be thinking about buying yourself a multi-million-dollar house in a very select part of your city. You may also be thinking about a new expensive automobile, maybe a great car like my Ferrari 512TR. Or how about throwing in a motorcycle, like my BMW R1200C Independent, taking a great holiday, and a million other fun things? Purchasing some great pieces of jewelry, or nice things for the parents and children? Some money for charity and the rest in a bank account and other investments, to give you interest every month and guarantee you a good lifestyle. You must be having fun dreaming and the reason is, you have connected pleasure to money.

Believe me when I tell you, that this same good fortune can also be connected to pain. US$10 million cash! What taxes do you have to pay your Internal Revenue Service? What about jealousy from other siblings, cousins; maybe even your father does not like you anymore! Remember, you are the only heir named to this fortune. I do not know about your country but I can assure you that in many countries, if you have US$10 million, you and your family are going to lose a certain amount of freedom. What about fear of kidnapping and extortion from criminals? In some Asian countries, it is normal for rich men to keep concubines and have second wives. Connect this money to the pain if you are the wife!

5. Workshop

a) Connect pleasure to marriage.
b) Connect pain to marriage.

I think you get the idea now that we can connect anything to pleasure or pain by choice. However, we have to remember Rule No. 4, in that everything we do in our lives is driven by our fundamental need to avoid pain and our desire to gain pleasure. We must therefore train ourselves to link whatever is important to us with pleasure, or we will self-sabotage ourselves to avoid pain.

I have good news for you. You can even link things you think are painful or not good for you to pleasure. Studies have shown how advertising companies use pleasure to sell liquor and cigarettes, which taste bad and are not good for you, to create billions of dollars in sales a year, by using pain and pleasure. What they have done, is to connect cigarettes and liquor to youth, beauty, success, health, outdoors, freedom, etc. Study some of the advertisements when you are watching TV, which I hope is not too often, as you want to be a leader in MLM. I had a great time one afternoon, watching a lengthy TV advertisement use the pain and pleasure principle to sell bras to women. My housemaids may have thought that I am some sort of pervert, but I can tell you that the advertising company were obviously good at what they do, associating pain to the woman not wearing their bra, and pleasure and happiness to the minute they use their product, and how well endowed they now are because of the bra.

How to successfully lose weight

If you are a little obese, want to lose some weight and think losing those extra pounds is important to you, you must not forget what you have learnt here. You must connect dieting to pleasure instead of pain, if you want to be successful, and you must connect food to pain, not pleasure. If you want to fail, all you need to do is to connect dieting to pain, and while you may lose a few pounds, your success will only be temporary, as when you have reached your goal weight, you will go back to pleasure, which is food, and gain back all those pounds again.

6. Why

Why am I spending so much time on this section, and using this exercise to close Book 1? My purpose is very simple. I want you to ask yourself how important your MLM business is to you. If you think it is very important and you desire success, you must train yourself to link pleasure to all the things you do in your MLM business. Link pleasure to sponsoring, retailing, public speaking, late nights, driving long distances, rejection, the need to phone downlines, uplines and customers, etc., all by injecting positive emotions. Lie to yourself if you have to, and never let negative emotions take automatic control and connect these activities to pain.

Workshop

a) List all the pleasures you think you will get if you become successful in your MLM business:

_____

_____

_____

_____

_____

_____

_____

_____

b) Now list all the pains you will get if you fail in your MLM business:

_____

_____

_____

_____

_____

_____

_____

7. The three keys to help you control your negative emotions

There are three keys to help you unlock the door that leads to the world of positive thinking and pleasure. When you are in your negative state or mood, what you must do is to interrupt this state, instead of letting your mind continue on its present negative track, unless of course you like that state and do not think change is necessary. It is just like playing your CD and when it is playing a negative track, having two choices:

a) Continuing to play the negative track, because you like the song.
b) Jumping track to another song.

If you want to jump track from your negative state to go into your positive state, you interrupt your negative state by using these three keys:

The 1st key is your Physiology

Your emotion and physiology is connected. What this means is that when you are in a certain mood, your breathing, facial muscles, body muscles and posture, also express themselves in certain ways which relate to that state of emotion. When you are happy, the physiology you use is different from your physiology when you are angry. So you have different physiology for all moods: when you are sad, proud, lying, fearful, confident, passionate, frustrated, etc., and because they are connected, it follows that you can use your physiology to influence your emotions.

Put your hands up, look upwards and put a big smile on your face. Now try thinking of something negative. You will not be able to do so, simply because this is positive physiology.

Let us imagine that you get a visit from a friend, and this person is the most negative person in your town. When he rings the doorbell, you happen to be in the shower and cannot answer the door immediately, so you shout and ask him to give you a minute, but for him to sit down on the chair in your foyer. This very negative friend sits down on the chair. Let us guess his physiology:

> Are his shoulders upright, or drooping?
> Is he looking up, or looking down?
> Is his breathing shallow, or deep?
> Is he smiling, or is there is no smile on his face?

How come you got the right answers? Guess what, you will also get the same answer in any country or with any ethnic group of people you try this on. We all have the same answer, because these are the physiology of a negative person when they are in their negative mode.

Whenever you want to jump track, to go from the negative mode to the positive mode, you can easily do this by:

200

a) Changing the way you move or posture.

b) Changing your breathing.

c) Changing your facial expression. You have over 80 muscles on your face, which control and can express many emotions. Remember the saying, "it is all written on the face."

d) Changing your physical fitness, so that you are healthier and have more energy.

The 2nd key is Language

The words we use to express ourselves also express our beliefs and emotions. Just by changing what you say, will immediately help you jump track. Try saying:

a) "You are mistaken" vs. "You are wrong"

b) "What can I learn from this?" vs. "Why I am so unlucky"

c) "This is the challenge" vs. "This is a problem"

d) "Maybe I should understand that we all come from different backgrounds" vs. "I don't like his character"

e) "Why is he so insecure?" vs. "Why is he so proud?"

f) "Maybe I should try to understand what he really wants" vs. "I don't like what he said"

g) "How can I improve my training, to make it more interesting?" vs. "My downlines have poor learning attitude"

h) "How can I teach my downlines how to retail?" vs. "My downlines are poor in retailing"

i) Instead of quarrelling with someone who is angry with you, choose instead to ask them what they want, or how you can help them. When a person is angry, it is really a cry for help, so when your spouse is angry, try this, "How can I help you Honey?"

I would like you to imagine the following scenario. A husband is in the washroom and after finishing what he has to do in there, discovers that there is no toilet paper in the holder. So he calls out to his wife for help. The wife cannot quite make out what he wants. Imagine the three different responses the wife may give, and see if you can feel the different emotions being expressed when:

a) The wife ignores the call. She can't even be bothered.
b) Rudely and loudly shouts, "What?"
c) Lovingly answers, "Give me a minute Honey."

Isn't it wonderful, that we can change our negative state of mind just by changing our language or the way we talk, rather than just letting negative emotions take control of our lives? So at this time, I would like to advise those who say things too quickly and regret later, to put a good 'ABS braking system' on their tongue. Think and change their language before speaking. Do not make the stupid excuse of saying, "I did not mean what I said." When you have to use this excuse, it is normally because you have said something bad, and let me assure you that you meant what you said in the first place. A passage in the Bible puts it very well, "The good man brings good things out of the good stored up in his heart, and the evil man brings evil things out of the evil stored up in his heart. For out of the overflow of his heart his mouth speaks." Better to keep what you mean in your heart, as you are in a people business.

On the subject of language, let me remind you of the importance of making a habit of using positive words instead of negative ones, because in the relationship between the conscious and the subconscious mind, you can control the subconscious mind by using auto suggestion. If you have the habit of saying negative things or words, you are using auto suggestion to influence your subconscious mind on negatives, and if you train yourself to say positive things or words, you are also influencing your subconscious mind on the positive. Both are just as powerful. So say something over and over again, with emotion, intensity and belief, until it becomes an incantation and the effect on the subconscious is like self-hypnotism.

Story: Boy and sugar

A boy was very comfortable, sitting in the living room watching the TV. The mother asked him to go to the kitchen to get some sugar and because he did not want to do it, he shouted back, "I don't know where the sugar is." The mother requested again and he replied again," I don't know where the sugar is." The mother then got angry and sternly ordered him to get the sugar. He got up but was angry because he did not want to do the task given to him. On the way to the kitchen, he again said, "I don't know where the sugar is."

When he got to the kitchen, he did not try very hard to look for the sugar and shouted again," I don't know where the sugar is." At this point, the angry mother went to the kitchen herself and found the sugar, which sat on the shelf right in front of the boy.

The reason why the boy could not see the sugar was because of his incantation," I don't know where the sugar is. I don't know where the sugar is." Even though the jar of sugar was right in front of him, he could not see it because he had self-hypnotized himself.

The 3d key is Focus or Belief

Your feelings stem from your focus or belief as you evaluate any given situation. Let us see how you feel if I tell you, "My grandfather, whom I love very much, passed away last night." When I do this during my training, I often hear students say, "Oh!" I can also see the sad and uncomfortable look in the eyes of many. I bet you feel the same too.

Now let me say the following, "My grandfather, whom I love very much, passed away last night and left me US$10 million in cash." Guess what? The, "Oh!" changes to "Wow" or "Yes!" I even see many smiling, apparently very happy that my grandfather died!

What happened? They have re-evaluated the situation and changed their focus or belief. You too can change your focus or belief in many situations and all you need do, is to ask yourself sensible questions. When you are down and depressed, why not ask yourself if things are really that bad? Are there others, whose problems are even more serious then yours?

Story: The Cross room

The young man was at the end of his tether. Seeing no way out, he dropped to his knees in prayer. "Lord, I can't go on," he said, "I have too heavy a cross to bear."

The Lord replied," My son, if you can't bear its weight, just place your cross inside this room. Then open that other door and pick out any cross you wish." The man was filled with relief. "Thank you, Lord," he sighed, and did as he was told.

Upon entering the other door he saw many crosses, some so large that the tops were not visible. Then he spotted a tiny cross leaning against a far wall. "I'd like that one, Lord," he whispered. And the Lord replied, "My son, that is the cross you just brought in."

Story: A true story that happened in Taiwan in 1995

A wife bought some mangoes for her husband when she went to the market. After dinner, she served the husband the mangoes, but the husband gave his wife a scolding, because the mangoes were not totally ripe. He shouted, "You stupid woman, don't you even know how to choose mangoes?"

The wife got angry and threw the whole plate of mango at the husband and she angrily shouted back," You ungrateful dog, I bought and prepared the mangoes for you, and you still scold me."

At this point the husband got up and slapped the wife. "I am your husband, how dare you throw the mangoes at me?" The wife took a knife and stabbed the husband in the chest and he died on his way to the hospital.

204

Let us examine the physiology, language and focus of the situation:

a) The wife bought some mangoes for the husband when she went to the market. After dinner, she served the husband the mangoes. No problem there.

b) The husband gave his wife a scolding, because the mangoes were not totally ripe. "You stupid woman, don't you even know how to choose mangoes?"

    Note the language.

    What do you think is his focus or belief? I guarantee you this is not the first time he called her "Stupid"

    Imagine his physiology?

c) The wife got angry and threw the mango at the husband and said, "You ungrateful dog, I bought and prepared the mangoes for you and you still scold me."

    Note the language.

    What do you think is her focus or belief?

    Imagine her physiology?

d) The husband got up and slapped the wife and said, "I am your husband, how dare you throw the mangoes at me?"

    Note the language.

    What do you think is his focus or belief? It is no longer the sour mango issue. It is now a "Who is the boss?" issue.

    Imagine his physiology?

This couple should have attended my training. I would have helped them be happier people and the husband might still be alive today!

Be aware of your own physiology, language and focus when you are doing your MLM business. It is a peoples business and as a business person in a people business, you should never let your focus and language run out of control. That is immaturity.

Maturity

Maturity is the ability to control anger and settle differences without violence.

Maturity is patience. It is the willingness to pass up immediate pleasure, in favor of long-term gain.

Maturity is perseverance, the ability to sweat-out a project or situation, in spite of heavy opposition and discouraging setbacks.

Maturity is the capacity to face unpleasantness, frustration, discomfort and defeat, without complaint or collapse.

Maturity is being big enough to say, "I was wrong." And, when right, the mature person need not experience the satisfaction of saying, "I told you so."

Maturity is the ability to make a decision and stand by it. The immature spend their lives exploring endless possibilities and doing nothing.

Maturity means dependability, keeping one's word and coming through in a crisis. The immature are masters of the alibi. They are the confused and the conflicted. Their lives are a maze of broken promises, former friends, unfinished business, and good intentions that somehow never materialized.

Maturity is the art of living in peace with what we cannot change; the courage to change what should be changed, and the wisdom to know the difference.

"Things do not change; we change." - Henry David Thoreau

8. Conclusion:

Why do we spend so much time on this topic, and use this topic to conclude our Book 1 training? The reason is in the fact that everything we do in our lives is driven by our fundamental need to avoid pain and our desire to gain pleasure. So unless you know how to link pleasure to your business, you will most likely quit this great business opportunity one day, and when that happens, you need not even bother to read Book 2 when it is ready, and probably have already wasted your time reading this Book 1. Training yourself to be a positive person and like what you are doing, will be the most important foundation of your MLM business. You must want to be here, you must like to be here, you must love to be here. Better still, go a little crazy and be a paranoid in your MLM business. If you really want to know why I am good in this business, it is because MLM is my life, my passion, and I choose to feel this way. I am a paranoid. You can be too. Learn to be a master of your emotions and recreate your identity, as Lao Tzu puts it so well, "He who controls others may be powerful but he who has mastered himself is mightier still."

Outline for Lesson 14
Positive thinking and pleasure

1. Introduction

Are you happy?
MLM is a people business. Negativity will turn people off.
Negativity also effects others:
Spouse and children
Parents or in-laws
Colleagues at work
Business associates in MLM business

2. It is a state of mind, not the blessings you received

Heaven and hell is between your two ears.
We are all born with two lives: one we are born with, and one that we can change.

Leslie Cheung

Carolyn Bessette

3. The source of positive and negative thinking

We have seven major positive and negative emotions.

4. The five rules that govern our mind and these two kinds of emotions

Rule No. 1

Our mind functions automatically. It will not remain idle.

Rule No. 2

Negative emotions come voluntarily. Positive emotions have to be injected. Air vs. Water

Rule No. 3

Positive and negative emotions cannot occupy the mind at the same time.

Rule No. 4

Everything we do is driven by the need to avoid pain or our desire to gain pleasure.
In the battle between pain and pleasure, pain will normally win.

Rule No. 5

We can connect anything to pleasure or pain, by choice.
Connect pleasure and pain to money.

Workshop

Connect pleasure and pain to marriage.
Train to link what is important to pleasure or you will self-sabotage.

How to successfully lose weight

6. Why

In your MLM business, is important to you link pleasure to:
Sponsoring
Retailing

Public speaking
Late nights
Driving long distances
Rejection
Phoning downlines, uplines and customers
Attending meetings, training and rallies
Home meetings and Product Parties

Workshop

a) List all the pleasures you will get if you become successful in your MLM business.
b) List all the pains you will get if you fail in your MLM business.

7. The three keys to help you control your negative emotions

The 1st key is your Physiology.

Your emotion and physiology is connected. You have different sets of physiology for different moods.

The 2nd key is Language

The words we use to express ourselves, also express our beliefs and emotions.
Change our negative state of mind, just by changing your language.
Control your tongue.

The Bible passage which says,
> "The good man brings good things out of the good stored up in his heart, and the evil man brings evil things out of the evil stored up in his heart. For out of the overflow of his heart his mouth speaks"

Make a habit of using positive words instead of negative words.
Auto suggestion
Incantation, saying something over and over again with emotion, intensity and belief

Story: Boy and sugar

The 3rd Key is your Focus or Belief

Story: The Cross room

Story: A true story that happened in Taiwan in 1995

Maturity

8. Conclusion

Link pleasure to your business or you may quit; go crazy and be paranoid in your MLM business.

Learn to be a Master of your emotions and recreate your identity to suit the role.

> "He who controls others may be powerful but he who has mastered himself is mightier still" - Lao Tzu

LEADER'S INCANTATION

I AM A LEADER

I WILL BELIEVE, NOT DOUBT

I WILL BUILD AND CREATE

I WILL LEARN AND TEACH

I WILL LEAD BY EXAMPLE

I WILL KEEP MY FOCUS

I WILL AIM HIGHER

I AM A FORCE FOR GOOD

I AM THE MASTER OF MY EMOTIONS

SEE YOU AT THE TOP

And God said, "No" to a Multi-Level-Marketer

I asked God to give me a big organization
and God said, "No."
He said He gives courage
and it is up to me to build it.

I asked God to give me knowledge to build this organization
and God said, "No."
He said He gives wisdom
and it is up to me to learn.

I asked God to take away my pride so that I will learn
and God said, "No."
He said it was not for him to take away
but for me to give it up.

I asked God to give me happiness
and God said, "No."
He said He gives blessings
but happiness is up to me.

I asked God to make my spirit grow
and God said, "No."
He said I must grow on my own
but He gave me a 'Book' to guide me.

I asked God to help me love my associates
as much as He loves me.
And God said,
"Ah, finally you understand Multi-Level-Marketing."

Wait for Book 2. Love you all,   EDDY

214

Notes:

Notes:

Notes: